45 YE
AN EASTBOURNE BUSMAN

1972-2017

Mick Hymans

Heathfield Publishing

FRONT COVER PHOTO:
Leyland Atlantean GHC521N originally bore the fleet number 21 but had been renumbered 30 on its return from Topline when photographed on the seafront in 1989. (Alan Snatt)

TITLE PAGE PHOTO:
Soon after delivery of the first batch of Atlanteans, the union had a dispute with management over their use and refused to drive them. For a short while they were all parked side by side in the bus park next to the depot. (Author)

REAR COVER PHOTO:
Stagecoach No.18174, about to leave Tunbridge Wells on the way back to Eastbourne, is a 2004 Dennis Trident with Alexander bodywork. (Mark Lyons)

Also by Mick Hymans: *A History of Eastbourne Buses*, The History Press, 2011

Photographs in this book not otherwise credited are by the author or are from his collection.

First published 2018

ISBN 978 1 85414 420 1

Published by Heathfield Publishing in Heathfield, East Sussex

Printed in the EU

CONTENTS

These AEC Regent IIIs were sold just before I started working on the buses, but I travelled on them on many occasions – often with my father driving.

PREFACE

Hopefully this book will be different to any of the books on buses you may have read before. It is not a book packed with details of engine sizes, seating capacities, coachbuilders or other technical details. It does intend to show though how being a busman has changed over the last 50 years from being an enjoyable job with a great social life to one which is governed by strict rules.

The 1970s sit-com "On The Buses" was not a million miles from being an honest account of the goings on at depots. My father had driven buses in Eastbourne during the 1960s and if he had not done so, then I probably wouldn't have wandered into the depot in Churchdale Road, Eastbourne searching for a job. It was only supposed to be a temporary position while I found better employment, but that never turned out to be the case.

There were numerous occasions when someone at work would say "You could write a book about this place." They were right. On retiring in early 2017 one of my colleagues put the idea of writing my memoirs to me. I started writing a few notes and as I wrote more stories sprang to mind until over 27,000 words later I had finished. Most of the images are unpublished and many come from my own collection, but I thank all the photographers credited for their work.

Mick Hymans

EARLY CAREFREE DAYS

I was born in Eastbourne in 1952 and have lived here all my life. I attended Hampden Park Infants School before progressing to Highfield Junior School. I was fairly bright and stayed in the "A" stream throughout my four years there coming in the top five in most exams and passing the dreaded 11-Plus. My main memories of this school though were being able to sit in the classroom and watch a steam engine shunt the small goods yard at Hampden Park Station three times a week. I returned to the school after about 50 years when it was hosting a model railway exhibition. The view to the sidings had long been spoiled by an estate of factories and a shopping centre. The classrooms and corridors looked much as I remembered them though. The walk to school had always been entertaining, as I would meet a group of train-spotting pals by the level crossing and watch the 08.20 West Country Class steam engine pass through on its way to Hailsham from Eastbourne. If we were feeling daring we would wait until it returned at about 08.55 which gave us 5 minutes to run to school before we were marked as being late.

My move to Eastbourne Grammar School changed all that. I don't know if it was because I had to have nine weeks off school with a kidney problem about three weeks into my first term there but I never got on at the school. Most of my teachers didn't even recognise me when I returned from my sickness and I remember one teacher having a very puzzled look on his face when he noticed me before he asked who I was. Anyway after laughing and joking my way through the next five years, I was the only pupil in my year to emerge from the fifth form without a single "O" level and on my final report the headmaster wrote that he could see no reason for me to return! I agreed and, in September 1968, I left.

That came as a bit of a blow, although it was not entirely unexpected. It was while reading a national newspaper a couple of days after receiving these results I came across an advert for vacancies in the civil service with the headline "GCEs OR NOT". "That's for me," I thought. I applied for an application form and it duly arrived. I filled it in and noticed that it stated the time and place that entrance exams were being held in London. I duly attended one Thursday only to be told that I should have waited until I had been given a date to attend and not just turn up! However, they allowed me to stay and found me a spare paper – which I passed. I had become a clerical assistant. Not exactly a title to impress young teenage girls!

AEC Regent III No.47 was used for driver training and was seen passing the Queens Hotel on the seafront. No.42 was sold to The Eastbourne Regent Preservation Society and can still be seen at many bus rallies.

Bus No.49 was the first of the AEC Regent Vs to be delivered and was in very clean condition when seen in Terminus Road. (Geoff Morant)

I was assigned to the prison officer department in Romney Street about 15 minutes' walk from Victoria Station. Every prison officer had a file which was split into up to seven sub-sections dealing with sickness, conduct etc. I'd never seen so much paperwork. I was responsible for making sure that other civil servants were given these files when they requested them. Most of the work done by the department could have been done locally at the prisons just as well and far more efficiently. For instance, if a prison officer needed time off for any reason, the clerks at his prison had to write to the Home Office to ask permission and a nondescript clerk in London would make the decision and write back to the prison. This was before the advent of emails and it seemed to me that the decision could have, and should have, been made at the prison.

There was a locked metal cabinet in the office that housed the "Confidential" files and only the office manager, Mr R, held the keys to this. One day when he was away, one of these files was requested by a more senior civil servant and a young lady who was his deputy opened the cabinet. The number of the file requested was listed on

An offside view of the same vehicle from this attractive and much loved batch.

top of a locked box inside the cabinet, so she found the key and opened it. The contents of the box surprised her and amused the rest of us – it was full of girly mags and bottles of spirits. I don't know who split on us but a couple of days after Mr R's return a memo was circulated saying that the box in the cabinet must never be opened again!

In those days we were still paid by cash and the money was brought from another Home Office building in Horseferry Road, just round the corner. The person who brought it to our office block had to get a taxi from the rank outside his building. We all felt sorry for the cab driver who had been queueing patiently on his rank to get his next fare only to be rewarded by a journey of 200 yards at the most. To add insult to injury, he was barred from getting a tip!

I soon realised that the civil service was not for me especially as £4 5/- of my £8 10/- take home pay went on train fares. My commuting days only lasted about 9 months and I found a job in the cost office at a local builders, Walter Llewellyn and Sons, who also allowed me to attend college one day each week. I managed to get 6 "O" levels.

In 1956 five more AEC Regent Vs were delivered in white with a blue stripe beneath the bottom deck windows and blue mudguards. They were also were fitted with translucent panels in the roof to make the upper deck brighter and were bought primarily to be used along the seafront. Full drop down windows were operated by the conductor with a "T" key. Staff were given cards with the times to open and close the windows. (Geoff Morant)

The next batch of AEC Regent Vs were delivered in traditional blue and yellow livery. These arrived in 1962 and were numbered 61-65. No.65 is pictured outside the railway station heading towards the depot at Churchdale Road.

The last batch of AEC Regent Vs to be delivered were Nos. 66-70 which arrived in 1963. This bus was to be involved in probably the worst accident in the Company's history when it smashed into The Lamb Inn, Old Town in 1965.

At 08.30 on the morning of 22nd June 1965 No.66 was travelling through Old Town towards the town centre when it clipped the back of a Southdown coach going in the opposite direction. The driver lost control and ploughed into the Lamb Inn. Miraculously no-one was killed.

Buses lined up between Platforms 3 and 4 at Eastbourne Station on a Saturday afternoon and waiting for the train of pensioners to arrive so they can be taken to their holiday accommodation. The blue van on the extreme right was the department's Austin LDO van which was mainly used to transport the takings to the bank but was used here to take any suitcases that would not fit on the buses. (Phil Clarke)

I'm not sure why I left them but I think it could be because I had got an old school chum a job in the office and found out he was getting paid 10/- (50p) a week more than I was. When I questioned the office manager about this, he told me that the difference was because he had a German "O" level – totally irrelevant to the position – and he refused to give me a rise.

Another move ensued and I became the time clerk at Edwards Instruments, which was part of British Oxygen. It was a bit of a dead end job and my office was on the shop floor whereas the accounts office was upstairs and the two trainee accountants always gave an air that they were better than me, but I put up with it as I was still getting day release to attend college where I was studying for my ONC in Business Studies.

During one spell of hot weather, many of the factory workers were complaining that there were no cold drinks available – only tea or coffee from the machine. Well, part of my duties was to hand out and retrieve time sheets on a daily basis, so one day I handed out suggestion forms as well. No-one ever put anything in the suggestion box which was opened religiously by the Managing Director's secretary every Monday morning. This particular morning, when she opened the box which was screwed to the wall of the machine shop, about 60 forms cascaded out, all demanding a cold drinks machine!

The local union officer was called into the Works Manager's office and he was told that it a gross misuse of the suggestion scheme. We never got our cold drinks but at least they never found out who organised it.

After gaining my ONC in Business studies with credit, I decided it was time to move on and handed in my 4 weeks' notice. Plenty of time to find a better job, I thought. Unfortunately not! I went for an interview at the Charles of the Ritz perfume factory in Burgess Hill, about 20 miles from Eastbourne and remember the interviewer with a grid on the paper in front of him. He asked me if I had theoretical knowledge of profit and loss accounts, balance sheets, bank reconciliation statements and a list of other accounting practices. I confidently answered that I did and he filled the first column of his grid with ticks. He then asked me if I had practical experience of the same things and he filled the second column of his grid with crosses. Needless to say I didn't get the job. No-one had told me it was a good idea to get practical experience while studying.

At the end of my four weeks' notice and still having not found a new job, I decided that drastic action was called for. I don't know why – maybe it was because my father had been a bus driver in the 1960s, but I wandered into the offices of Eastbourne Borough Council's Transport Department bus depot in Churchdale Road and

A conductor ably demonstrates the dangerous practice of leaning out of the bus to change the side blind.

No.66 was rebuilt after the Lamb Inn accident and served for many more years but never seemed to be "quite right". The radiator cap used to grind against the bodywork when cornering. It was eventually converted into a recovery vehicle and renumbered 98. It was pictured next to sister vehicle No.67 inside Churchdale Road depot. It has since been preserved.

applied for a job. I was given an application form to fill in there and then. Name and address was easy. Height? Hmmm – not sure. About 5'8" I suppose. Near enough. Colour of eyes? Much trickier. Didn't have a clue. I was just trying to see my reflection in the office window when a manager walked in saying "I hear you've applied for a job as a driver/conductor."

"No, not driving. I can't drive a bus" I replied.

"How old are you?" he asked.

"Twenty" I said. "Twenty-one in about six months"

"That's perfect. Conductors have to work here for six months and then we put them in the driving school. Can you start Monday?"

And I did.

I reported at 8am on Monday 12th September 1972 and was introduced to Dennis Willoughby who was the Training Inspector, not only for conductors, but also for drivers. He took me down to his training room which was in the basement of the new office block that had been added to the original depot. One of the training devices he had for drivers was a "state of the art" simulator. This consisted of a mock-up of a Ford Anglia driving seat and controls. The "road" you drove down was a small model of a country lane inside the machine with a small camera suspended from the top of the model. As you

In 1966 allegiance was switched from AEC to Leyland and 10 PD2s, Nos 71-80, were purchased. The first of these, No.71, was used as a training bus and was the bus I learnt in and passed my test in. Pictured behind it is the Leyland Panther Cub No.92. (Peter Henson/OS)

drove round, the model moved and the image the camera saw was projected on to a screen. More of this later.

Training would take a week with Monday and Friday spent in the depot and the other three days out on the road with another conductor. Part of the first day was taken up with getting fitted out with a uniform – both summer and winter variety. The winter uniform consisted of a heavy black serge jacket with yellow piping round the collar and the letters E.C.T.D. embroidered on the lapel. The ends of the sleeves were trimmed with leather cuffs with the right hand one having a white stripe so it showed up better when doing hand signals. The trousers were made of the same heavy material with yellow piping down the outside of each leg. An even heavier overcoat was also supplied. A peaked cap was an optional extra. The summer uniform was much lighter both in weight and colour but still had the same letters on the collar. Buttons on both uniforms were detachable and bore the town's insignia bearing the legend – *Meliora Sequimur* – meaning "We Follow the Better Things." The rest of the day was taken up with learning the department's rules and regulations and how to work the Setright ticket machine.

The conductor I was assigned to for my training was RP, a young hippy type who had worked there for a couple of years. The thing

Another of the first batch of PD2s No.72 was used as the reserve driving school bus. It was pictured here in Trinity Place with an AEC Regent V in the background.

Another 5 PD2s were purchased in 1967. These were virtually identical to the first batch but could be identified as their side indicators were placed above the cab rather than behind it. For some unexplained reason No.83 was also given a smaller fleet number beneath the cab window.

that distinguished Roger, apart from his long hair and dry sense of humour, was the length of the strap he had on his Setright – it was nearer his knees than his waist! He was a very good conductor though.

He told me that four out of five people who are running for a bus only want to go two or three stops – and the fifth one .... it's the wrong bloody bus anyway! And it's true. People who need a bus that runs every thirty minutes or hourly make sure they are at the stop before the bus. Those who have the luxury of a five or ten minute service wander out to catch the first bus that comes along. A good example of this was a service to Jevington we used to operate. There were two return trips each week – one on Tuesdays and one on Thursdays to take the villagers shopping in Eastbourne. The locals valued their service and were always polite and pleased to see us. Compare that with areas of the town that enjoy a bus every ten minutes and listen to the moans if they have to wait any longer.

Parked in Ivy Terrace and waiting for drivers to return them to the depot were PD2 No.82, now preserved by Stagecoach, and Dennis Dominator No.43.

No.84 was open topped in 1973, given a coat of pale blue paint and christened "The Seafront Sunbus". The side windows were removed in 1985.

I soon learnt that it was the conductor, rather than the driver, who kept the bus on time. Some conductors would finish serving a passenger before ringing the bell, but good ones would make sure they were "on the bell" at stops and ring it as soon as the last person's foot had left the rear platform or had boarded, being ready with a strong arm round their waist to stop them falling backwards as the bus pulled away.

With training over I was let loose on my own. At that time about half the services were still crew operated and the rest were one man operated (yes we were still allowed to call them one man buses then – there were no female members of staff and political correctness had not been invented, when they had to become one person operated.) The busiest routes were still crewed using AEC Regent Vs or later Leyland PD2s. The crew rota was split into two shifts – early and late – with drivers moving down one line each week whilst conductors moved up one line. This meant that a crew stayed together for a week and they got to know each other fairly well before moving on. One of the first things that struck me was the different atmosphere to office life. No-one was trying to impress the bosses for promotion. Everyone was friendly with nothing to prove.

We all worked an 8 hour day 5 day week with hours ranging between 05.40 and 23.59. There was a canteen that was open from 09.00 until 19.30. There were always at least two card schools on the go with the favourite game being Black Mariah which was played for pennies to make it more interesting. There was also a games room next to the canteen that housed two snooker tables and a dart board. Both of these were usually shrouded in cigarette smoke as the habit had not been banned in those days. I couldn't complain, because I was contributing to the unhealthy atmosphere as much as anybody else.

There was always plenty of overtime going. Rush hour buses were operated by "extras" and there were about ten of these in the morning and seven in the evening all covered by overtime. A normal day for the young single staff was to work a morning extra, then meet in the canteen for a coffee and cake or burger and game of cards before killing time before our duties started with a game of putting at Princess Park or working on our cars, many of which really shouldn't have been on the road – not by today's standards anyway!

The ex-Blackpool PD3 was numbered 81 into the Eastbourne Buses fleet being the 2nd PD3 to bear that number. The previous one had been withdrawn in 1981. (Alan Snatt)

SERVICE 1

LANGNEY and OLD TOWN (Eldon Road Circular)

SINGLE FARES
(Stage numbers shown in brackets)   **FOR DENTAL ESTIMATES BOARD FARES—SEE PAGE 17**

(24)	LANGNEY (Marsden Road) or LANGNEY RISE (Martello Inn) (24)
(25)	2	PRIORY ROAD (Williams Court) (25)
(1)	2	2	LANGNEY ROUNDABOUT (1)
(3)	3	3	2	ST. ANDREWS (Norway) (3)
(4)	3	3	3	2	ARCHERY (4)
(5)	4	3	3	2	2	WHITLEY ROAD (Seaside) (5)
(7)	4	4	4	3	3	2	LEAF HALL (7)
(8)	5	5	4	3	3	3	2	SEASIDE ROAD (Terminus Road) or PEVENSEY ROAD (Susans Road) (8)
(9)	5	5	5	4	4	3	2	2	EASTBOURNE RAILWAY STATION (9)
(10)	6	5	5	4	4	3	3	2	2	ENYS ROAD (Upperton Road) (10)
(11)	6	6	6	5	4	4	3	3	2	2	TOWNER ART GALLERY (Lambe Inn) (11)
(12)	6	6	6	5	5	4	4	3	3	2	2	TALLY HO! (12)
(14)	7	6	6	5	5	5	4	4	3	3	2	2	BROOMFIELD STREET (Green Street) (14)
(16)	7	6	6	5	5	5	4	4	3	3	2	2	VICTORIA DRIVE (Eldon Road) (16)
(14)	7	6	6	5	5	5	4	4	3	3	3	2	2	WILLINGDON ROAD (Eldon Road) (14)
(12)	8	7	7	6	6	6	5	5	4	4	3	3	2	2	OCKLYNGE (Selwyn Road) (12) or MILL ROAD (Prideaux Road)
(11)									4	4	3	3	2	2	MOAT CROFT ROAD (Upperton Road) (11)
(10)									4	4	4	3	3	2	PRINCESS ALICE HOSPITAL (10)

OTHER SINGLE FARES
(24) LANGNEY (Marsden Road) or LANGNEY RISE (Martello Inn) and Lodge Inn (Seaside) or WINSTON CRESCENT (2) ... 2p
(2) LODGE INN (Seaside) or WINSTON CRESCENT and CHRIST CHURCH (6) 3p
(4) ARCHERY and TERMINUS ROAD (Langney Road) or LISMORE ROAD (17) 3p

A page from the 1971 fare chart – the first one to be in decimal coinage.

A page from a timetable, also from 1971, showing the frequency of buses on the main route through the town.

1

OLD TOWN (Eldon Road Circular) —
EASTBOURNE STATION — ARCHERY — LANGNEY

1

MONDAYS TO FRIDAYS

OCKLYNGE (to Old Town)								0700	0710	0722	0734	0746	0758	0810
CENTRAL AVENUE				0634		0655	0705	0715	0727	0739	0751	0803	0815
TALLY HO!				0637		0659	0709	0719	0731	0743	0755	0807	0819
EASTBOURNE STATION				0645		0705	0714	0725	0737	0749	0801	0813	0825
ARCHERY	0555	0619	0639	0649	0654	0713	0714	0723	0734	0746	0758	0810	0822	0834
MARSDEN ROAD (via Priory Road)*	0559	0623	0643	0653	0700	0717	0720	0729	0740	0752	0804	0816	0828	0840

then continuing as for weekdays below

SATURDAYS

OCKLYNGE to Old Town			from Newick Rd	0700	0715	0730		0745	0800	0810	
CENTRAL AVENUE				0634	0655	0705	0720	0735		0751	0803	0815 and con-
TALLY HO!				0637	0659	0709	0724	0739		0755	0807	0819 tinuing
EASTBOURNE STATION				0645	0705	0715	0730	0745		0801	0813	0825 as for
ARCHERY	0555	0619	0639	0654	0714	0724	0739	0754	0800	0810	0822	0834 weekdays
MARSDEN ROAD (via Priory Road)*	0559	0623	0643	0700	0720		0745	0800	0805	0816	0828	0840 below

WEEKDAYS

OCKLYNGE to Old Town	0822	0834		0858	0910	0922	0934		0958	1010	1022	1034		1058
CENTRAL AVENUE	0827	0839	0851	0903	0915	0927	0939	0951	1003	1015	1027	1039	1051	1103
TALLY HO!	0831	0843	0855	0907	0919	0931	0943	0955	1007	1019	1031	1043	1055	1107
EASTBOURNE STATION	0837	0849	0901	0913	0925	0937	0949	1001	1013	1025	1037	1049	1101	1113
ARCHERY	0846	0858	0910	0922	0934	0946	0958	1010	1022	1034	1046	1058	1110	1122
MARSDEN ROAD (via Priory Road)*	0852	0904	0916	0928	0940	0952	1004	1016	1028	1040	1052	1104	1116	1128

*Buses continue to terminus at Langney Rise (Martello Inn).
For other buses between Old Town and Eastbourne Station see Service 2 (p.14).
For other buses between Eastbourne Station and Langney see Service 4 (p.24).

Terminus dep.	Service No. and Route	Mart. dep.	Arch. dep.	Stn. dep.	Destination arr.	Terminus dep.	Service No. Route and destination	Stn. dep.	Arch. dep.	Mart.	Other Destination arr.
		-	-	-	-	-	1-LDSC direct	-	0544	0548	0550
0551	2-Sks-O.Tn.-Farl.Rd.	0555	0601	0615	0625	0627	1-O.Tn.-LDSC direct	0640	0649	0654	0657
0704	4o-S'ks-Ock-Eldon Rd	0709	0716	0727	0734	0735	1-O.Tn.-Martello.	0745	0754	0800	-
-	1-O.Tn.-Eldon Road.	0806	0813	0824	0832	0838	4-Ock-Martello.	0848	0858	0906	-
-	4A-Mill Rd-Eldon Rd.	0913	0920	0931	0940	0941	4E-O.Tn.-Pool-Botany	0951	1001	1009	1016
1018	4E-Pool-Ock-Eld.Rd.	1025	1033	1047	1054	1058	1-O.Tn.-Martello.	1108	1118	1126	-
-	1A-O.Tn.-Filch.Rd.	1134	1141	1152	1202	1206	14B-O.Tn.-Wink.F.E.	1217	1227	-	1236
1239	4H-Ock-Hosp.	-	1250	1301	1310	1313	4-Ock-Martello.	1324	1334	1342	-
-	1-O.Tn.-Eldon Rd.	1350	1357	1408	1416	1420	4A-Mill-Mars.F.E.	1431	1441	-	1450
1457	4-Ock-Eldon Road.	-	1506	1517	1524	1527	1-O.Tn.-Martello.	1537	1547	1555	-
-	1-O.Tn.-Eldon Road.	1606	1613	1624	1632	1638	4-Ock-Martello.	1648	1658	1706	-
-	4A-Mill Rd-Eld.Road	1713	1720	1731	1740	1741	4E-O.Tn.-Pool-Botany	1751	1801	1809	1816
1818	4E-Pool-Ock-Eld.Road	1825	1833	1847	1854	1900	14-O.Tn.-Parkfield	1910	1919	-	1930
1937	1-O.Tn.-Eldon Road.	-	1947	1958	2006	2006	4-Ock-Martello	2015	2024	2030	-
-	4-Ock-Eldon Road.	2033	2040	2051	2058	2100	14-O.Tn.-Parkfield	2110	2119	-	2130
2137	1-O.Tn.-Eldon Road.	-	2147	2158	2206	2206	4-Ock-Martello	2215	2224	2230	-
-	1-O.Tn.-Eldon Road.	2233	2240	2251	2259	2259	4-Ock-Archery.	2307	2316	run in.	

AVAILABILITY OF CONCESSION FARES: Monday to Saturday - 0913 at Martello until and including 1201 at Central Avenue. 1357 at Archery until and including 1615 at Whitley Road. 1759 at High Pavement until and including 2205 at Drive Hotel.

A set of Running Sheets were issued to all crew members. These detailed what every bus was scheduled to do from the minute it left the depot until it returned.

At the back of the Running Sheet booklet were the "Extras". These were the buses that just went out during the morning and evening peaks. These days, in Eastbourne at least, these do not exist and the standard service copes at peak periods.

1st EXTRA

MONDAY - SATURDAY

0720 Archery (Ser 14) to Brodrick Road (Pulborough Ave)

0732 Pulborough Avenue (Ser. 14A), 0733 Henfield Road, 0735 Parkfield Ave., 0740 Hydneye to Station (G.Rd)

0808 Station (Ser. 9) to Brodrick Road, via Brassey Avenue.

0820 H.Pk Station, Ser 9, Depart in front of service bus. 0825 Henfield Road, 0827 Willingdon Park Drive (Friston Ave) to Seaside Road.

At Railway Station change destination to Ser 4A and continue to Marsden Farm Estate.

0902 Marsden Farm Estate via Priory Road (4A) to Station

Run in private.

NOTE FOR ALL EXTRAS

Check Extra Duty Sheet daily for variations.

All journeys via Station to Seaside Road operate via Bolton Road.

2nd EXTRA

SCHOOL DAYS ONLY

Ex Depot Spare as detailed until:-

0805 Archery to Trust House via Lottbridge Drove

0818 Trust House, Ser 9, via Brodrick Road and Lindfield Road to Memorial Square.

0841 Station (G.Rd) to Meads (Wellcombe Crescent) (College days only)

Private to Gildredge Road.

0858 Station (G.Rd) to Meads (Wellcombe Cres). Show 'Private' destination. Only school children and teachers to be carried

3rd EXTRA

MONDAY - SATURDAY

0746 Archery to Marsden Farm Estate (4A) (Telscombe Road)

0756 Marsden Farm Estate to Station (4B)

Private via Kings Drive.

0825 Parkfield Avenue (14A) via Freeman Avenue, Hampden Park Station, Hydneye (dep. 0830) and Lottbridge Drove to Station (dep. 0846), Ooklynge and Central Avenue.

Then as detailed.

My first car had been a Sunbeam Rapier which cost £3 from the local car auction. I remember the insurance cost me £66 – 22 times as much as the purchase price! Another car I had was an Austin Cambridge which really should not have been on the road. It broke down one day and on inspecting it, we realised that there was no fuel getting through to the carburettor from the electric fuel pump. After fiddling about with it to no avail I turned the ignition off and my mate, MT, who had his head buried under the bonnet shouted. "It squirted some through then" I turned the ignition back on and another squirt was projected from the detached fuel pipe although it didn't continue to flow. We reconnected the pipe. I turned the ignition on and off a couple of times and then tried to start it. Hey presto! The engine burst into life. But it was short lived. It soon ran out of fuel again. The solution was obvious. Keep turning the ignition on and off while driving down the road making sure that at junctions and crossroads there was enough petrol in the carburettor to get over the hazard by turning it on and off 3 or 4 times in quick succession. If this wasn't bad enough, it would not stay in top gear unless held there with a strong left arm. It also had a bad steering wheel vibration at about 40 mph. Driving this car was not exactly relaxing. It entailed driving along with one hand on the gearstick while being shaken to pieces while constantly turning the ignition on and off, but I put up with it for a while before trading it in. I actually swapped it for a packet of 20 cigarettes with another driver at work and I think I got the best deal!

Another area of life that people had a completely different attitude to in the early 1970s was drinking and driving. It was perfectly acceptable and many happy hours were spent in the pub both before and after work. The Archery Tavern, now sadly demolished, at the junction of Seaside and Churchdale Road was the busmen's' local. Pubs had very restricted opening times then – from 1030 until 1430 at lunchtimes and 1800 until 22.30 or 23.00 in the evening. For those crews working a late turn when the canteen was shut, the Archery was a good substitute. Meal breaks were only about 40 minutes long on average, but long enough for a pint or two. It was quite common for a crew to enter the pub and announce what bus they had just come off outside and the crew taking it over would drink up and go. Most drivers were sensible but one or two did have a drinking problem and ran up a tab all week and spent nearly all their wages, paying it off on a Friday before starting again. One driver, JC, would come to work with a bottle of wine in his pocket, and pull the cab blind down behind him so passengers could not see him taking the odd swig. These days no-one would work with such a person, but back then no-one had any qualms about working behind him. I certainly didn't.

To allay anybody's fears, it doesn't happen these days. Drivers are subjected to strict random drink and drugs tests. Anyone failing is dismissed. A few years ago before the company had its own testing kits, an inspector thought he could smell alcohol on a driver's breath. He let him take his bus out but called the police. By the time they caught up with him, he just passed their test and was allowed to continue. A while later though, he was stationary taking fares in a shopping centre at Langney when his bus was hit by a 4 x 4 towing a mobile food wagon. The wagon was completely demolished blocking the entrance to the centre. The police were called and the driver of the 4 x 4 was breathalysed. He passed. They then breathalysed the bus driver because he had been involved in the accident. His luck had run out this time and he failed. He was rightfully dismissed. I digress!

No.92 was a Panther Cub used by Leyland as a demonstrator. In 1967 it was loaned to Eastbourne and returned to them but in 1968 it was purchased and returned to Eastbourne. Elderly passengers hated it as it had a very high entrance step. It was withdrawn in 1979 and sold to Rollinson, a dealer in Carlton.

No.86 was a Daimler Roadliner new in July 1967. It proved to be very unreliable but it stayed in service until the end of 1978 and it was sold early the following year to Booths, a dealer in Rotherham.

In 1968, three of these Leyland Panthers with East Lancs bodies were bought. They proved to be more reliable than the Daimler Roadliners of a similar age. No.87 was sold to Ongar Coaches in early 1984.

Drinking nearly cost me my job though. One day, I had a long conducting turn to do starting about 15.00 and had had a few pints in a town centre pub before getting in my car and driving to work. I had not got far when I got involved in a very minor accident and to my shame did not stop. Instead, noticing the time was about 14.20, I thought I had just got time for a quick one in the Archery Tavern to calm the nerves. MW was sat at the bar. I ordered a pint and told him of my accident. He asked how much damage I'd done and I confessed I had no idea. We went outside and the only damage was a small mark on the rear bumper. "That'll come off" he said rubbing it. "Don't bother" boomed a voice from behind. "I've caught you already." I asked the gentleman if he had informed the police which he said he hadn't. I pleaded with him not to as I was in the driving school and said I would pay for any damage to his van. We exchanged details and he left. When I came off the road for my break a policeman was waiting to see me. He asked if he could see my car. I was not keen on this because I had hand painted it about 10 different colours, which had made it very easy to spot parked directly outside the pub! Anyway it was now parked on a car park opposite the depot and I led the officer to it and showed him the damage.

No.91 was one of two Daimler Roadliners purchased in 1968. They spent more time in the garage than on the road and were sold in 1977 – this one to Carlton Metals.

"Are you sure you hit him?" he queried. "There's no damage to his van."

"Well," I said, "if you're not so sure then nor am I."

"He's got a witness though" said the officer.

I admitted "Well, in that case, I probably did."

He was a decent copper and told me that he was glad I had been straight with him otherwise he would have thrown the book at me. In the event I was fined £15 for driving without due care and attention and had my licence endorsed. Now that presented me with a problem. The court case was held on a Monday and I was due to take my bus driving test that Thursday and I needed my licence back! Luckily I had the time and the cash to pay the fine and retrieve my licence.

Now some of you will remember driving licences when they came in the form of a little red book. The validity of the licence was on the first page while any endorsements were put in the back. Came the day of the test and Mr.Vidler, the examiner, asked for my licence and he just checked the front page. I then proceeded with my test, which I was convinced I had failed, so much so that I gave a thumbs down sign to a driver I passed when nearing the depot at the end

In 1970, 10 new single deckers were purchased. These were Leyland Panthers with East Lancs bodies. They served the town well before they were all sold to the Bexhill Bus Company in 1984 although they only used a couple of them for spare parts.

Driven by the guy I went through the driving school with, Leyland Panther No.8 sits outside the Seven Sisters Public House on Hamlands Estate. This was just outside the Borough Boundary and in Southdown territory which explains the bus stop plate. Weekly season tickets that were valid throughout Eastbourne were not valid here. This caused many arguments with passengers and much time was wasted trying to explain to the many foreign students who were staying with families in the area that they had to pay to get to the Borough boundary.

of the test. After answering a few questions on the Highway Code I was told I had passed! Dennis, the instructor was ecstatic. He had not had a failure in the last 7 or 8 he had taught so was sure that either Ivor, who I was in the driving school with, or myself, must fail. We had both passed. I was asked for my licence again. This time Mr.Vidler checked the endorsements at the back and looked somewhat amazed at the one dated three days previously. He glared at me and I just smiled and shrugged. What else could I do? In my defence that was the one and only endorsement I ever got.

A sequel to the story was that the van driver was an upholsterer with his own business. A few years later when I had married, I returned home from work only to find the wife choosing some fabric to have our settee recovered and it was the same upholsterer she was doing business with. I think he recognised me. I certainly recognised him. When he had left I protested that there was no way I was going to put £300 of business his way. It turned out I was wrong as she liked the material she had chosen and I remember her saying something to the effect it was my own stupid fault!

Before a new driver could go on service by himself, he had to have type training – about 20 minutes driving of any type of vehicle on the fleet. Then he was issued with a float card. New drivers had to drive every route with another experienced driver and this card was a simple document that recorded routes driven and time taken. If the regular driver was satisfied that the bus had been driven safely he would sign the card. When all the routes had been driven, the float card was handed in and you were eligible to drive on your own.

The crews were always playing tricks on each other. On some crew buses, in order to change the front destination screen, the driver had to open a small flap in the roof of his cab so he could see what blind was showing. Upstairs there was an access panel to the blinds, and if a conductor had a "T" key he could open this and balance articles on the flap which would cascade into the cab when opened. A favourite with some was to balance a plastic cup of water on the flap. On other buses the driver had to put his hand through the flap to reach the handles that wound the blinds up or down. One conductor was lying in wait and grabbed his mate's hand nearly giving him a heart attack. Conductors were not immune from practical jokers. One conductor always left his ticket machine in its metal box at the bottom of the canteen stairs. On one occasion his ticket machine was replaced with a brick and he only discovered this after he had taken over his bus and rang his driver away from the stop.

One conductor, FR, was well known for his sense of humour. He had worked there for years and even conducted behind my father in the 1960s. He was one for the ladies and always enjoyed pushing his

No.9 ended its life in Eastbourne as an information bus and was painted in the experimental primrose/brown livery. After it had been sold to the Bexhill Bus Company it became a mobile café.

The "Exact Fare Please" sign was on the front was because an Autofare system was being trialled. The ticket was issued from a machine just behind the driver which is just visible in this image. No change was given to passengers without the correct fare and the experiment ended without being adopted for future use.

way through a standing load getting a grope on the way. He knew that you could be as cheeky as you liked with people providing you kept a smile on your face.

One day, he had a few minutes stand time at the railway station and took the opportunity to go to the loo on the platform. On his way back to the bus, he noticed there was no-one in the barbers shop on the concourse so he nipped in for a quick short, back and sides. When he got back to his bus, an inspector asked him where he had been. He told him and was duly reported to management. At his disciplinary hearing he was again asked by a manager where he had been.

"For a haircut," said Frank.

"A haircut!" said an enraged manager. "You don't have a haircut in the firm's time."

"Why not?" replied Frank. "It grows in the firm's time."

"Not all of it," said the manager.

"I never had it all off," quipped Frank.

The frustrated manager just told him to get out and Frank had got away with it again!

What a state! The white and blue livery did not wear well and No.17, pictured at Birch Road was badly in need of a repaint. The bus behind did not look much better.

All bus companies have to have spare drivers to cover sudden sickness, breakdowns and accidents. I was working one of these duties that clocked off at 21.30. If you weren't needed, there came a point when you could not be used, so you could normally get away early. On this particular evening about 20.40, I decided to call it a day, but started chatting to another colleague in the doorway. I had my coat on with bag over shoulder and was in full view of the control inspector, who was sitting in his office. I was stood there chatting for at least 5 minutes before I left. After I had gone, this inspector put a call out over the tannoy for me and then walked round the depot to make sure I had gone. He then put in a report stating that I had left early. Now, if he had needed me for a bus changeover or something similar, that would be a "fair cop" and no complaint from me, but to sit there knowing I was going to leave and not say anything, is to my mind, just plain nasty. I have never had any time for those who have been prepared to get others into trouble to further their careers. But I was to get my revenge. About two weeks later, I was on the same duty and the same inspector was in the office. At the time I went home previously, I asked him if it was OK to go home. He said it wasn't, so I went back into the canteen.

A couple of minutes later he came looking for me. I went home bang on time. The following night I was working one of the last buses to run in and this inspector was also working late. I had a private hire to do though, which was to pick up a party of caravanners who were having a party in one of the seafront hotels, and take them back to their caravans. They did not need picking up until 01.00. I sat in the duty room reading a book. When everybody else had gone home, this inspector told me to leave as he wanted to lock up. I pointed out that I was still working. "Yes, but I want to go home" he said. I pointed out that he did not officially finish until 00.15 and it was still only 23.45. He was enraged! He telephoned the manager, DS, to tell him. I was hoping he was asleep in bed but he must have been out as he did not answer his phone. So he then phoned the Chief Inspector, JB., who did pick up the phone. The CI wanted a word with me. I pointed out that this inspector was willing to wake him up and get him out of bed to tell him he was not able to go home 30 minutes early which is what he had booked me for two weeks earlier! I had never seen anyone foam at the mouth before but this inspector was. Having made my point, I let him go home, but I was not exactly flavour of the month with the whole inspectorate for a couple of weeks.

One of the original Leyland Atlanteans, No.16, was the first of a long line of buses to be given an all over advert. This one for PST Travel was hand painted with flags of different nationalities and was spotted on a private hire.

Three of us were spare one evening and I had got hold of a Ouija board. To pass the time we thought we'd try a séance. We set it up in the canteen and after a while in response to our question "Is there anybody there?" the upturned glass moved to "Yes". We looked nervously at each other and I then asked "Have you got a message for anyone?" At that precise moment the tannoy boomed "Driver Hymans to control please". We all jumped out of our skins and never tried it again.

The Transport Manager when I started was a Mr. Leach. I don't have too many memories of him as he soon resigned and his deputy, Mr. Doug Sissons was promoted to his position. He was a great Eastbourne United Football Club fan, as was the shop steward, SD. My over-riding memory of DS had nothing to do with work though. One winter's morning he ventured into his back garden and slipped on a piece of ice, falling over and breaking his leg. His cries for help were heard by a neighbour who went to his rescue, slipped on the same piece of ice falling over on to DS's leg, breaking it again, with the second break being worse than the first one.

Licensing laws in the early 1970s were fairly strict. Pubs had to shut at 11.00pm. Private clubs were allowed to stay open later, but only if they supplied food. There was a club in Carlisle Road called the Woodville Theatre Club, affectionately known as "The Woody" and catered mainly for those attending or appearing at the nearby theatres but welcomed bus drivers who had been working late and we were normally given a bite to eat free to comply with the law. Most single busmen working late at weekends headed for "The Woody" after work. I left there one night about 01.00 with MT and we decided to get something to eat. Now, this was in the days before lots of fast food outlets existed and as pubs shut before midnight, so did any eateries. After driving round Eastbourne in his old beige Hillman Minx without finding anywhere open, we refused to be beaten and carried on driving. We were eventually successful when we found a burger stall open at Thornton Heath, South London at around 03.00. We arrived back home just as the milkman was delivering our milk.

On another occasion on leaving the club with RK, he said that we could try to make some easy money. "How are we going to do that at this time of night?" I asked. "Taxi service" he said. Thinking that was a great idea I pulled up on the rank outside Eastbourne Station. An elderly lady climbed into the back of my old estate car and asked to be taken to Lewes! It turned out that she had boarded the train at Brighton and fallen asleep missing her stop and her last train back. We fended off some awkward questions like why was there

Recovery vehicles at work. Above the Land Rover is sent to Ramsay Way to attend to a Leyland Atlantean and, below its successor, 98 prepares to tow another one in from Terminus Road.

The next few images show how cramped the conditions were at the Churchdale Road depot compared to the new premises at Birch Road. Above: An Atlantean has its gearbox removed. Below: Cluttered workbenches.

two of us, why we had busmen's uniforms on and where we were going when we had to stop to relieve ourselves behind a hedge! We delivered her safely and probably cheaper than a proper cab. She showed her appreciation with a handsome tip.

With pubs all turning out at the same time there was always a rush for the last bus home. At that time the last buses all left the town centre for every part of the town at 23.00. Six or seven buses would all converge in town about 22.55 which gave any passenger who had to change buses time to do so. There would also be a spare bus in case of overloading or a breakdown. An inspector would also be standing with the buses and when he was satisfied that everybody had boarded, he would blow a whistle and the buses would take off in all directions. Any timing points were ignored after that and crews went flat out – as a policeman once put it "It was a touch of the Red Arrows." On more than one occasion the driver of a crew bus did not wait for his conductor to ring the bell and he just went on the whistle, but his conductor had been on the pavement chatting to someone or had nipped to the loo and had been left behind. He then had to ask the driver of the spare bus to give chase or run to the next stop where his driver would be waiting, fuming quietly. Taxi drivers at a nearby rank would occasionally blow a whistle before 23.00 and we would all leave early, even though we knew it was not the inspector's whistle, and then plead innocence when confronted by the inspector back at the depot.

Conditions for signwriting adverts weren't ideal either, having to balance on top of a step ladder.

One of these last buses to Old Town, which was one-manned, was normally quite full and quite often there was trouble on board. To try to combat this, another member of staff would travel on the bus. This was known as "riding shotgun" and seemed to quell any problems. Two hours overtime was paid to anyone volunteering to do this. One of the drivers, RW, had a better idea though. His wife would meet him just before he started the last trip and leave their large Alsatian with him. The dog would sit at the front of the bus just outside the cab door and "greet" the passengers as they boarded. He never had any trouble.

The crews rushed to get back to the depot as they had to pay their money in and with only one cashier on duty, a queue could form to cash in and valuable drinking time could be wasted. This was in the days when money had to be put into paper bags. £5 of silver would go into a beige bag and 5/- of copper would go into a smaller blue bag. These bags would then have to be weighed and any mistakes sorted there and then. Loose change had to be counted. Scholars could pay with prepaid paper vouchers and conductors who had been on a school run could have a pile of these that would have to be counted and logged. You did not want to get stuck behind a conductor with a pile of these.

The main bay for parking of buses with Regent Vs or PD2s reversed into bays at the side. The central bays were for the single deckers, so all of these had to be booked out before any in the side bays could be moved.

Next to the depot behind the office block was another parking area. Buses were reversed here after being refuelled at the main parking bay.

Another area became available for parking buses opposite the depot when the old destructor works were demolished.

Two views of the new depot under construction. Above The 10 lanes where buses are parked overnight and below the purpose built pit area which can hold 8 buses each with its own entrance door.

Believe it or not there were a small number of females who were attracted to our uniform. One of these ladies had been riding round on a bus all evening chatting to the conductor. She stayed on the bus until it ran in at the end of the night's work. He gave the girl his car key and told her to wait while he paid in. He excitedly told those in the duty room to hurry up because his luck was in. but was far from it. When he left the depot both the girl and his car had disappeared, never to be seen again! To add insult to injury it came to light that she had had difficulty in starting the car, and had asked a couple of drivers leaving the depot for a bump start and they were only too happy to help a lady in distress!

There was always a problem in employing and retaining staff, so in 1973 it was decided that clippies could be employed. They had kept the service running during the war years and it seems strange these days that there was a policy of not employing females. The first of the ladies passed her PSV test later in the year to become a driver.

In 1973 Idi Amin threw a lot of Asians out of Uganda and many found a new home in Britain. One of them came to work on the buses. He was living in a flat near the town centre. On some of the tea time rush hour buses there was enough time to grab a drink and he would invite his driver back to his flat for a quick cuppa. We were amazed. He had a large screen TV (by those days' standards anyway) and new furniture better than most of us had at home. He was also driving to work in a Vauxhall Viva while many of us were coming by bike or bus. He had not been able to bring any assets with him from Uganda and the British Government had given him and his wife £300 each and a smaller sum for each of his children.

One of these teatime buses was the 39th Extra which left the depot at 1600 and invariably was allotted the driving school bus that returned to the depot about that time. More often than not it was a rush to take off the "learner boards" that covered the destination boards and remove an "L" plate that was tied to the radiator grille with a piece of string. One day I was driving this bus and "accidently" forgot to remove this just to see passengers' reactions. I pulled into bus stops sitting up very straight and trying to look very nervous. Expressions on peoples' faces when they saw an "L" plate was interesting to say the least. One passenger told my conductor that she thought I was doing very well for a learner and another illogically said she did not mind paying for herself as I was learning but thought she should not have to pay for her dog.

On nice sunny days, it was most pleasant on the back platform leaning against the pole and watching the world, and pretty girls, go by. The conductor was in charge of two destination panels – one at the rear and one on the side. These were changed by turning a handle and a small viewing panel was set into the body so we could see what blind was displayed. Lots of us though would prefer to lean off the side of the bus whilst turning the handle. This was fine when stationary but potentially dangerous when on the move. The AECs had a blind for Langney that included Archery beneath. One conductor, BG had got into the habit of leaning out and winding off "Archery" as soon as he had passed it. He had repeatedly been told not to do this. One day, after ignoring the warnings, he again leant out of the bus, and his cash bag got caught round the wing mirror of a parked car and he was yanked from the platform and slid down the road on his face. He was badly injured but survived. I don't recall him returning to work.

Driving the old AECs and Leyland PD2s was very physical work. They were not equipped with power steering and with a good load on, became very heavy indeed. Turning right from Seaside Road into Cavendish Place often involved standing up and bracing your right knee against the steering column in order to get enough purchase to get round the corner. A shop next to the junction in Cavendish Place

In my view this batch of 1975 Leyland Atlanteans (18-25) were the shoddiest vehicles ever delivered. Many of the interior panels were simply riveted together with rivets showing. The 30ft long throttle cables had no grease points which made operating them very "notchy."

had a blind which when opened was very near the kerb and this was side-swiped on more than one occasion.

The AECs had fully synchromesh gearboxes whereas the PD2s had crash 1st and 2nd gears with only 3rd and 4th being synchro. For those lucky enough not to be old enough to remember crash boxes it meant that changing gear meant double declutching. A gearchange meant depressing the clutch pedal to take it out of gear, releasing it and then revving the engine so that it matched the road speed, depressing the clutch again before selecting the gear. If you got it right, the gear was selected silently and smoothly. If you got it wrong it would hurt your hand! The grating of the gears would reverberate back up the three foot metal gearstick and the gear knob would vibrate violently in your hand. Just as bad was the whole bus would know you had got it wrong because the noise it made could be heard throughout both decks. One place where 3rd to 2nd was always required was going up Rodmill Hill. I had a tried and tested way for doing this. The PD2s were flat out in second gear at 15 mph so going up the hill I waited until the speed had dropped to 17 – 18 mph, took it out of gear then floored the throttle before sliding it back into gear at 15 mph then dropped the clutch with the throttle

Another early one man vehicle was this Seddon Pennine purchased in 1973 to replace the AEC Regal No 93. It had to be returned to the manufacturers for modifications to the brakes but they were never safe. It was sold to Cardiff City Transport in April 1977.

Old and modern side by side. The Seddon stands next to No.93, an AEC Regal III of 1950 vintage. It was sold for preservation in 1978 to Miles of Greenford but re-acquired in September 1992. It is now owned by Stagecoach and repainted in original blue/yellow livery.

still wide open. The take up was smooth and you stood a good chance of getting to the top of the hill without changing down again. Some drivers let their speed drop before changing gear and they lost momentum which invariably meant repeating the same procedure from 2nd to 1st which was more risky. Part of the driving test was to change from 3rd to 2nd while going down the hill. This meant partially applying the handbrake to maintain an even speed while changing gear.

Most buses pulled away happily in second gear so there was only one place where using first was needed. This was pulling away from the Tally Ho! public house in Green Street. Going from 1st to 2nd meant doing a "snatch change". This involved pulling away in 1st and then in one swift movement the clutch was dipped and the gear lever swept as quickly as possible from 1st to 2nd. Failing this hurt your hand again, and meant stopping and trying again. I remember one day, when smoking was allowed whilst driving, I was in the middle of executing this change when my cigarette fell from my lips onto my seat and rolled back towards me! Panicking, I stood up to avoid getting burnt and missed 2nd gear badly. I managed to stop the bus while still standing up, retrieve the cigarette and carry on. It was a bit of a hairy moment though.

During 1978/9 another 8 Atlanteans, 28-35, were purchased. These were longer, being able to seat 82 passengers compared to 76 on the original ones.

For a short while I used to bring a cassette recorder to work and have music playing in the cab. I had to have it on fairly loud to drown out the sound of the engine throbbing away next to me. You can't play Status Quo quietly anyway, can you? One passenger remarked to my conductor that she thought it was a good idea that music was now being piped around the buses! The AECs had a nice flat top to the wheel arch in the cab, but the arches in the PD2s followed the curvature of the wheel which meant balancing the player was a bit trickier. Traversing a roundabout one day it slipped from the wheel arch and lodged beneath the throttle pedal and I had to try to extricate it whilst winding the lock into the other direction.

While on the subject of stupid ways that accidents can happen, I got into my Mk1 Ford Cortina one day outside my house and drove off down the road as I had down on numerous other occasions. But this time my right leg wouldn't reach the brake pedal and the junction was coming up fast. My immediate thought was what had gone wrong with my leg. I stopped the car by braking with my left leg. Heart pounding somewhat, I looked down to see that my shoelace had caught in the door when I closed it. When I accelerated it had undone my lace which was not long enough to reach the brake pedal.

In the mid-1970s decorating buses as all-over adverts was popular. This Atlantean was painted to represent a music centre popular at the time. Some duties required drivers to leave their bus parked in Ivy Terrace, near the station, and another duty had to pick the bus up and return it to the depot, but it was not unknown for the driver to forget to bring the bus back. Another driver then had to be dispatched to retrieve it. One night about 23.15 a call was taken from the police to ask if we were aware that this bus was still parked in Ivy Terrace. The inspector on duty thanked the officer, then looked to see what driver had forgotten to bring it back to the depot, only to discover that it had not been booked out that day and it had been there over 24 hours and no-one had missed it!

Another all over ad was No.33 for the Ship Inn in Meads Street. A reception party of management and brewery officials was waiting at the pub to receive the newly painted vehicle, but unfortunately nobody had thought to check it had been re-fuelled and it ran out of diesel on the way there.

Nos. 28-35 were long wheelbase versions of previous Leyland Atlanteans. No.28 was one of two converted to fully automatic – the other was No.31 - photographed leaving Langney District Shopping Centre sporting an advert for a local furniture store.

Another of the long wheelbase Atlanteans to be given an all over advert was No.30 advertising Sir Speedy exhaust systems.

In 1981 Eastbourne Buses switched their allegiance from Leyland to Dennis and four Dominators Nos 38-41 were purchased. No.38 received an all over advert for Hampdens Furniture Store in 1988 and carried it for four years. It was sold to Ensignbus in August 1994.

Shoelaces are dangerous though. I used to have a motor bike for a while and set off for work on my 650 Triumph. I stopped at a crossroads on our quiet estate to give way to an approaching car, but I had not noticed that the loop in my shoelace had wrapped round the gear lever so my foot wouldn't reach the road. I lost balance and just fell off with motor bike on top of me. The lady driving the car stopped and inquired if I was OK. "Fine" I replied but was struggling to free my shoelace now underneath the bike. Anyway, with only a bruised ego, I managed to eventually carry on.

Anyway I digress again.

Eventually the depot entered the 20th Century and installed a drop safe, thereby negating the need for a cashier to work late. The first day it was used, management were standing in the duty room instructing the staff on how their new pride and joy worked. All the takings were placed in a plastic bag which had a tag with a number stamped on it. A couple of steps had to be climbed to reach the shoot the money would drop into. The tag would then be placed into a special slot with the money placed into a device not unlike a drop safe and the cover pulled down. A button was then pressed, a gurgling sound would be heard, a receipt would be issued and the money would drop into the safe. Everything was working fine until CF, a cheery rotund Maltese driver, came in. He placed his takings in a bag, climbed the steps, placed the tag in the slot, pulled down the cover, but clung on to his takings. The machine gurgled away and printed a receipt. CF turned round and walked down the steps, receipt in one hand and takings held triumphantly in the air in the other. Management's faces were a picture!

We were still paid in cash as well. Before we could collect our wages we had to pay in any "shorts" we had accumulated during the week. Our money would then be handed over in a small brown envelope. It is this system that got me into my first serious trouble. We were paid on a Friday at 1pm. On this particular Friday I had taken a lieu day and gone to London to a model railway exhibition at Central Hall, Westminster, so did not pick up my wages. The following day, I did not clock on until 15.00. When reporting for duty I asked for my wages and was told by the inspector that he had put them in the drop safe at 13.00. I asked him why and he said it was in the rules that any wages not claimed by then would be put into the safe. "But you knew I was coming in," I protested. "It's still the rules," was the reply. I spent the rest of my conducting duty seething at this ridiculous statement and decided to that I would fight fire with fire, so in my paying in bag I just put a little note that said "You've got my wages, so I've got your takings". I then put their money into my locker which was in a purpose built locker room made entirely of breeze block with the only entrance being a solid wooden door which was locked overnight. When I reported for duty next, which was on the Monday, I discovered that management not only had no sense of humour, but no sense of justice either. I was to face disciplinary action for my sins. The deputy manager was a Yorkshireman, a Mr. L. He said that I had put their money at risk by leaving it in my locker overnight. I countered by saying that nobody knew it was there and the door was locked so it was perfectly safe. He disagreed. I said that it must be safe as that is where we were expected to put any takings when on a break. He said it was safer with the door open and people about. A sort of Northern logic, I thought. Anyway, he was not to be persuaded and gave me a final warning. I appealed his decision. The appeal was to be heard by the manager, Mr. S. His deputy, Mr. L and as we were still owned by the council, a man from HR at the Town Hall attended. I was represented by my shop steward. I decided that the best way to present my appeal was to put it in writing. That way I would not forget anything and there was less chance of losing my rag. I made enough copies of my defence to supply everybody with a copy except Mr. L .who sat looking quietly annoyed as everybody else read my submission. It was agreed that we were not arguing over whether I was guilty or not but over the severity of the sentence. It was commuted to a "caution" which I was happy with.

Men being denied their wages caused more problems in 1977 when the pay cheques never arrived. This was in the days before money was paid directly into bank accounts. It was in June, the week of the Queen's Silver Jubilee and staff at the Borough Treasurer's had had an extra day off and were late finalising the wages. Staff had not been warned of this and those who were on their day off and gone to the depot specially to get their money were becoming annoyed at having to waste their time waiting for their pay to turn up. Eventually an emergency union meeting was called and buses were taken off the road in a lightning strike so members could attend. And lo and behold within a couple of hours of this, the cheques were delivered and everyone went back to work.

On Saturdays during either end of the holiday season, a special train would come to Eastbourne full of old age pensioners on cheap holidays. This would be met by up to eight buses and these would be used to take them round to various local hotels. The scenes would be chaotic. About 300-400 pensioners would alight from the train and head for the buses that were lined up about three abreast under the canopy between platforms 3 and 4. Blackboards with the names of the hotels each bus was serving were placed in the rear nearside window. Most of the suitcases would arrive in the guards van and be offloaded onto station trolleys and wheeled round to the buses. The problem was that buses are not designed to carry large amounts of luggage. If you were lucky, you could fit three suitcases beneath the stairs but there could be about 30 or more for each bus. The solution was to turn over the two inward facing bench seats at the rear of the downstairs saloon and pile the suitcases high on them. If this was not sufficient, then any suitcases due to be dropped off at the first hotel were pushed down the aisle. Turning over these seats, of course meant that there were fewer left for people to sit on. And pensioners can't get up stairs. Or so they thought! After a stand-off between holiday makers and crew some of the more agile of them would eventually venture upstairs. One argument often made by the crews was that their hotel had a flight of stairs leading from the pavement to the foyer so if they couldn't climb stairs they could not stay there. The following Saturday morning, the whole process was repeated in reverse when they were picked up from hotels and returned to the station. It was mainly covered by overtime and you needed a lot of patience and a good sense of humour to work these but they were seldom short of volunteers.

In 1975, eight new Leyland Atlanteans were delivered with East Lancs bodywork and to my mind were very substandard and were very indicative of how far standards had dropped. I believe they had been standing for quite a while and the throttle cables had virtually seized up. These cables were about 30ft long and devoid of any greasing points. Normal pressure on the throttle had no effect; the pedal wouldn't move. More pressure had to be applied before the cable would grudgingly give way with more throttle than wanted normally the result. I believe our mechanics introduced greasing nipples along the cable length alleviating the problem. The finishing on the inside was also not very good. The bulkhead at the front had a large square panel simply riveted on. A shortage of foglights meant a later batch, 28–31, were delivered with plastic discs covering the space where the lights should have been.

No.29 was an ex-Colchester Leyland Olympian with ECW bodywork, seen in Kings Drive on 23 March 1991. (Alan Snatt)

Like the first batch of Atlanteans, they had semi-automatic gearboxes, although they differed by being electrically operated rather than by air pressure. The air boxes had a problem in that they took a while to disengage gears, especially 1st and, to some extent, 2nd gears. This meant that you had to hold it in neutral before selecting the next gear, otherwise two gears which were worked by bands would enmesh together, causing damage. Both types were driven by a fluid flywheel where oil was injected against a large flywheel with about 20 veins. The pressure of the oil against the veins caused it to revolve, creating the drive. We were constantly told to use 1st gear when pulling away because pulling away in 2nd would cause the oil to break the veins rather than turn the flywheel and this led to poorer acceleration. These were used by Daimler on buses as early as 1930 and were seen as ideal as it ensured a smooth pull away from bus stops.

The delivery of new one man buses meant that more routes could be converted from crew operation. Although some of the older drivers preferred driving crew buses, most preferred one-man operation, mainly because it paid more. In those days it could take about five years until a permanent place on the one-man rota was achieved. Until then you never knew what you were doing from one week to the next – crew driving, one-manning or sometimes back conducting. In the summer months you could be assured of driving as student conductors were employed and they weren't all male either. There were some very nice female clippies and more than one liaison started which led to at least three marriages and I know that two of them are still going strong today. They weren't all totally suitable for working in very conservative Eastbourne though. One lass was very foul-mouthed and soon got to be nicknamed "Liverpool Lil." She would often have the top two or three buttons of her uniform shirt undone and it was very obvious she did not wear a bra. Although the crews never complained, some passengers did and a rather embarrassed manager had to call her in to his office to advise her of the standards of dress expected.

In the 1970s many schools used to take their students swimming and used the buses to transport them to and from the baths. One of these pools was Motcombe Baths in the Old Town area of Eastbourne and off the route of normal bus services. It was reached by turning left into Milton Road from Motcombe Road, then right into Gore Park Road before turning right again into Bakewell Road so we could offload the kids outside the baths. One particular day on my first trip as I turned right into Bakewell Road, I saw that the Gas Board had dug a hole right in the middle of the road. A new yellow gas pipe

With the superb architecture of Eastbourne Station in the background, Dennis Dominator No.40 in mint condition enters the bus precinct.

came out of this hole from the right side and went to the pavement. On the left side was the spoil taken from the hole so I could not pass on either side. There were no workmen to be seen so I called my student conductor and told him that I had no alternative but to drive the bus over the top of the hole and asked him to keep an eye on things as I did so. I gingerly pulled forward but as I was completely over the hole, four Gas Board employees in their Land Rover came round the corner. I carried on and stopped outside the baths and the kids alighted. My conductor didn't follow me down the road but stayed there looking at the hole. "Come on," I thought, "Hurry Up. Let's get out of here". Too late! One of the men was running down the road. "You've squashed our pipe," he was shouting.

There was nothing that either of us could do. The damage had been done. On subsequent trips we reversed round the corner to pick up/drop off as we didn't think they'd be too amused if we did it again.

MORE SERIOUS TIMES

1976 saw major changes in my life when I obtained a wife, a mortgage and a sense of responsibility.

We were all part of the Transport & General Workers' Union. I had no interest in politics or how the union's hierarchy worked, but I was interested in the activities at the depot.

At one union meeting I remember that providing a Boxing Day service was being discussed and I brought up that, as only a handful of buses would be on the road, the crews should be able to have the relative luxury of using the new Leyland Atlanteans. At least they had doors on and decent heaters. This brought much opposition from the more senior drivers, who seemed to regard them as their own personal property. They said that we were not trained to drive them. I argued that the only person who could say if we were qualified or not was the driving instructor, DW. He agreed with me and they were used.

In 1984 the company wanted to change the livery to primrose and brown. Four buses were lined up in Hyde Gardens bearing alternative liveries and the public were asked for their opinion. Luckily the primrose and brown was rejected in favour or the aircraft blue/ biscuit livery applied to No.27. 1,200 people voted with the results being bus 27 – 478 votes, 32 – 132 votes, 67 – 116 votes and 68 – 413 votes.

The union chairman was NC. Nobby was a large imposing character who was not only chairman of our local branch, but also convenor for all the other municipal branches, e.g. gardeners, theatre workers in the town. Eastbourne is normally Tory but at times does have a Liberal MP and council but Nobby seemed to be on good terms with whoever was in power. This seemed a bit suspect to many of us especially as our management seemed almost scared of him. Some of us believed that he was a sort of "double agent". He never had to drive a bus, but had a cushy little job where he drove the staff bus early in the morning and took the previous day's takings to the bank in a van that nobody else was allowed to drive, even if he wasn't using it and a driver needed transport to get to a bus. He was also in charge of a small team of cleaners who had the nickname "The Untouchables". When, under the Transport Act of 1986, councils were not allowed to run their own bus companies, Eastbourne Buses Ltd. was formed as an arm's length company to the council. Nobby was presented with a watch at a social event to mark the occasion by the leader of the council who thanked him for all he had done for them. For them? He was supposed to be on our side! We also found out that he had been given a Mini Metro for his own use. He would not drive this into the depot but parked it around the corner. We were also suspicious that he was booking, and being paid for, overtime he did not do. Management flatly denied this. When working a late duty one night, an inspector who thought along the same lines as me decided to try to get some proof. We waited until everybody else had gone home and then went into the wages department and found about five or six of his recent clock cards that showed he had booked overtime nearly every day and been paid for it. I showed these cards to one of the managers who was more interested in how I had come by them. I told them they had been delivered in a plain brown envelope. Despite the evidence, the manager still denied he was being paid overtime. Most mysterious! More and more members were questioning his activities, so when he was due to be re-elected, I stood against him and won – and so began over 30 years of union activity.

The social life in the depot was good and most weekends a ballroom in one of the larger seafront hotels would be hired out for a disco. There was also an annual Busman's Ball that was held in a larger ballroom on Eastbourne pier and was open to the public. Even though it was held on a Thursday several hundred people used to attend.

The social club also had several sections. Apart from a darts and snooker team, there was also an angling section. Some of us

No.67 kept its trial livery until it was withdrawn and dismantled at the depot in 1986. The Atlantean had been bought second hand from Southampton City Transport.

who were keen on model railways asked if we could form a Model Railway section. There was a room accessed only from the south side of the depot and down some steps into a basement that had been used for storage, but was prone to flooding. We were told that if we cleared it out the old metal ticket machine boxes and other rubbish, we could use it. These boxes still contained dirty smelly water from the floods but eventually we made it a usable space. For our initial meeting, management allowed us to use the training room. After the business of the club, the driving simulator proved too much of a temptation to us though. It needed an ignition key to operate it and after rifling through some drawers and cupboards it was found in the top drawer of a filing cabinet. A couple of the drivers did some laps round the country lanes before PC, who was still a conductor, asked for a go. Well, why not? What harm could he do? After successfully negotiating a couple of bends he managed to drive off the road and up a grass bank. Unfortunately the miniature camera hit a bush, made from a piece of lichen, dislodging it causing it to roll down the bank and come to rest in the middle of the road.

We had no way of accessing the model to replace the bush, but we couldn't leave it in the road. We solved the problem by continually driving as fast as we could and running the camera into the bush until we had finally pushed it back up the bank. Our antics were never discovered. When the depot closed, the simulator was given to the local Air Training Corps. The model railway club prospered for a couple of years holding exhibitions in the town before we merged with the town's other, older established club which had better premises but a dwindling membership.

One vehicle on the fleet was a Land Rover that was used for towing in broken down buses. These days this would be totally illegal as the law has now been changed to say that the towing vehicle had to be heavier than the vehicle it was towing and then later to say that a tow bar was no longer good enough and buses must be lifted and towed.

In the middle of the dashboard was a metal lever that looked as if would operate an air vent, but it was in fact a hand throttle for a winch on the front. This lever overruled the accelerator and much fun could be had with new drivers who weren't aware of this. Pulling this lever across would cause the Land Rover to accelerate sharply, much to the astonishment of the poor driver. Pushing the lever back at the last moment caused many a brow to be wiped.

No.63, a Leyland Atlantean with ECW coachwork was one of the first second hand buses to be purchased. It was one of four that came from Ipswich Corporation in 1980. In 1985 it was converted to open top and in 1989 named *The Eastbourne Queen*. (For photo, see page 57). It was delicensed in 1992.

I was given a job one day to take some young schoolchildren to Exceat in the Cuckmere Valley where they were to go canoeing. I was allotted a Daimler Roadliner for the job. They were never reliable at the best of times and when I tried to start it, it was suffering from a flat battery – again! A mechanic was called and he jump started it. I did express my concerns that after sitting at Exceat for about three hours, it probably wouldn't start again. I was assured it would. It didn't! Luckily there was a phone box nearby – it was in the days before mobiles – and after a while I spotted the trusty Land Rover coming down the hill towards us. Another bus was sent to pick up the children. The mechanic took the tow bar from the back and told me of his intention to tow me back to Eastbourne. I refused point blank. For those who do not know the area, the road from the Downs into Eastbourne is a very long steep hill, about 1 in 8. With no engine running on the bus I had no power steering and no brakes and I was not going to rely on the brakes of the Land Rover to stop us. He then decided that the next best thing was to try to bump start the bus in the car park but he was not too optimistic. Now this car park is not tarmacked and gets very dusty in dry weather, which it was. It was also very busy with cars parked either side. Many of the car owners were sitting in folding chairs enjoying their picnic lunches and enjoying the spectacle of us trying to start the bus. We hitched the two together with the tow bar and we gently and slowly manoeuvred the bus to one end of the car park. Checking that it was all clear, the accelerator on the Land Rover was floored and the clutch dropped. Even the 4-wheel drive could not cope. Wheels spun and dust flew. Lots of it! Happy picnickers dived for cover inside their cars. Although it was a really amusing spectacle, you have to do your best not to laugh, don't you? Needless to say, the bus still wasn't going. Another call to the depot was made, another mechanic arrived – eventually – and jump started it.

The Land Rover was eventually replaced by a bus that had been converted to a breakdown truck. The bus in question was an AEC Regent V, No.66, which was the one that had crashed into the Lamb Inn, Old Town in 1965. The bus, although rebuilt, had never been "right". The radiator caps on these AECs came up through the bodywork next to the bonnet. After the accident, when cornering on this bus, the neck of the radiator would grate and bang on the bodywork. Mechanics tried to fix this by making the hole it came through bigger but it never worked and no matter how big they made the hole, it didn't cure the problem. It was eventually sold to a local scrap car dealer who kept it for a number of years before selling it on.

Another of the ex-Ipswich Corporation Atlanteans, No.65, seen here at the terminus at the Top of Beachy Head. No.66 was painted blue/cream and named *Eastbourne King*.

Another of the ancillary vehicles was an old Commer van which was used as a staff van which used to do a couple of laps of the town very early in the morning to pick up staff who did not have their own transport. This was part of a very cushy duty worked by a senior member of staff. There was a similar trip at night after all the buses had run in to take staff home. This was worked by overtime and was an easy way of earning two hours pay. More often than not, the person working it would use their own car and drop drivers off on their way home. Another use for this van was to take the previous day's takings to the bank. In those days it was very unusual for a note to be tendered for a fare so there were an awful lot of coins. These were placed inside a specially built cage for safekeeping. This cage rattled terribly and the noise was unbelievably deafening. In case the driver was attacked there was a switch the driver could throw which disabled the van. I think it blew a main fuse. This switch was clearly labelled "ONLY USE IN AN EMERGENCY" Many a driver's curiosity got the better of him and they flicked the switch! After trying in vain to restart the van they had no option but to make the embarrassing phone call to tell control what they had done.

This van was eventually superseded by a 25 seat Seddon Pennine for staff transportation purposes and contract work. Apart from being very unreliable, it was also lethal. The brakes were said to be the same as on a 32 ton artic. They could not be applied gradually like normal brakes. You gingerly pressed the brake pedal, then "Bang" – they were on hard. Several complaints were submitted from the Union and at one stage it was "blacked". The Ministry were called in to check the brakes and they put it on a rolling road, where it passed! Well, of course it passed, we protested. We're not complaining it does not stop, but it stops too quickly. The social club had two more sections – a snooker team and a darts team, and the management were good enough to let the teams use the Seddon for away fixtures in nearby towns. One night coming back from a snooker match in Seaford it skidded off the road. Nobody was injured but there was a lot of damage to the rear of the bus. After the workshops had rebuilt it, the darts team borrowed it for a match in Hailsham. Coming back from the match it skidded off the road again. Again no injuries but lots of damage. Soon after this, I remember early one rainy morning going to work on it. The driver was a likeable senior driver called Monty. He was saying that anyone who could not handle it should not be driving buses. As we approached a set of lights, they changed to red. Monty braked and the wheels locked up and we sailed through the lights on red. Monty changed his views after that. No-one was

No.168 was a Leyland National new to London Transport in June 1977. Eastbourne Buses acquired it in early 1987. It became No.12 in the fleet before being withdrawn in January 1991 and sold to a dealer. (Geoff Morant)

sorry when in March 1977, it was eventually sold to Cardiff City Transport, but we wondered how long it would last on wet hilly South Wales roads.

The design of the first batch of Regent Vs delivered in 1956 was slightly different inasmuch as the bonnet needed to be raised to access the radiator cap. This was sprung loaded on a clip hinged on one side. On many occasions, the driver whose job it was to fill them up in the morning would put the bonnet up, flip up the rad cap and fill it up. Having put the watering can back down, they would slam the bonnet shut, forgetting to close the rad cap first. Eventually this abuse started to warp the bonnets slightly so they would not shut properly. Normally this did not matter, but on windy days, the wind could get beneath the bonnet and it would start to lift. Sometimes it would just "float" neither up nor down before dropping back down or sometimes opening right up. It happened to me one day while driving along Lottbridge Drove (a long straight windswept road) and I thought there was no point in stopping to put it down as it would probably be blown up again. At the end of the road I had to turn right at a roundabout, so half way round I opened up with side cab window, stood up and leant out of the cab and pushed it down only to see a police car waiting to enter the roundabout. I was sure he would come after me, but luckily he must have had more urgent things to do.

Parking in Eastbourne had always been a problem.

This was partly due to lack of parking wardens and those on duty weren't exactly rigid in their enforcement of the rules. This caused me to have a couple of episodes. The town had for a while turned the bus stop boxes into Clearways and that had certainly helped with illegal parking but had not eradicated it completely. Before our route out of town had been altered, we used to stop outside Marks & Spencer in Terminus Road. Approaching this one day in a Leyland Atlantean, two vehicles were parked on the thick yellow line at the front of the stop. The front vehicle was a builder's pick-up truck. As I pulled round them, a taxi in front of me went to pull up on the stop. "Oh no, you don't," I thought and pulled in relatively sharply and gave him a blast on the horn. He pulled away again but I had taken my eye off the back of the bus and the rear nearside had come to rest leaning on the pick-up's front wing scratching his paintwork. I was livid! Mainly with myself. Up until that moment I had managed over 25 consecutive years without a blameworthy accident. I noticed a traffic warden coming towards me, but when he saw the accident he turned round and started walking away. I had to chase him down the road. When I caught him up he told me that he had given the

A Scania with East Lancs bodywork was loaned to Eastbourne in July 1981 for a short period.

builders permission to park there. As we both walked back to the accident I pointed out that they could have parked opposite and he had no right to give them permission to break the law. By this time the owner of the pick-up had returned and he was not happy. That made two of us! We exchanged details and then the warden asked me to move the bus. We were on a one-way street and nobody could get past. I refused to move the bus as it would cause more damage to both bus and pick-up. He said he would have to call the police. I didn't mind as I thought it was about time someone made a stand about the parking problem in the town so I invited him to do so. While we were waiting a member of the public informed me that he had seen the builders coming from a café carrying cups of coffee. The warden still refused to give them or the car behind a ticket. The police could not get to us through the traffic so had to drive through a pedestrian precinct to reach us. I explained the situation including why I was so irate. They were understanding but still would not hand out any parking fines even though I asked them what you had to do in the town to get a ticket. They asked me to move the bus but again I said if I did I would cause more damage than already done. I must admit that a little bit of me wanted to get in the bus, put it on a full lock and floor the throttle, ripping his wing off and then blaming the police as I was just carrying out their instruction, but I didn't. Instead the builder was made to climb over his passenger seat and put his vehicle on a left hand lock and drive up onto the pavement. I then continued on my way, receiving my first "blameworthy" accident report from management a few days later.

The second incident happened on the main road between the town centre and Langney, known as Seaside. This is the widest road in the town, but double parking often reduces it to one lane. One of the worst culprits used to be the owner of an auction who would double park his Volvo Estate (much loved by antique dealers) even if there was a parking space a few yards away. I had lost count the number of times I had been held up by it. One morning going into town, I noticed it double parked again. Returning about an hour later, it was still double parked but all the cars legally parked by the kerb had gone, leaving the Volvo "abandoned" in the middle of the road. I must have been having a bad day, because I lost it – big time. I left the bus and stormed into his premises shouting "Who owns that ****** Volvo parked in the middle of the ****** road out there?" He was not amused and pushed me out of his shop. I told him if I saw it double parked again I was going to let his ****** tyres down. He followed me onto the bus and demanded my name. I ignored him and got onto the two-way radio to inform the depot of the situation. By this time a lady in the front seat was getting a bit impatient and asked when we were going to leave. My uninvited guest who was fiddling with his mobile phone then stated that he was perfectly capable of standing up on a moving bus. I thought "Suit yourself" and pulled away with him leaning against the windscreen. He then spoke into the phone with words I will never forget. "Yes Police. I've been kidnapped by an aggressive bus driver!" Well, I really thought I'd blown it. I stopped at the next bus stop and opened the doors. Looking in my mirror, I noticed another bus right behind me. I signalled the driver to stop as he passed and I asked the rather bemused driver to make a mental note that I was stationary with the doors open and the gentleman was free to leave if he wanted to. With that he got off and started walking back to his business. I set off again and a couple of minutes later I passed a police car with a blue flashing light with one of our inspectors in hot pursuit in the company's Escort Estate. They found the gentleman concerned who was admonished about his parking and for pushing me from his premises. I heard nothing more about it. A couple of years later I walked into another auction room in town and came face to face with him. We both recognised each other but said nothing.

Two Ipswich standard Roe bodied Atlanteans were received at the same time as an Olympian in exchange for the four Dodge/East Lancs minibuses and were pressed into service still in Ipswich livery. No.96 was seen at Eastbourne Arndale Centre passing the Station on 2nd July 1987 while on loan pending the exchange. (Alan Snatt)

Years later, parking in Eastbourne was decriminalised and parking charges introduced. Private wardens were employed and illegal parking improved immensely, but amazingly, the new wardens have no jurisdiction in Terminus Road bus precinct although it is still part of the public highway. The situation may alter however, because as I write this, the Arndale Centre is being extended and the road layout will change.

The two way radios were one of the best additions to the buses. We originally had the ability to communicate with other buses as well as the depot, but due to misuse by drivers chatting to each other, normally on quiet winter's evenings, this ability was disabled and we could only hear messages from the depot. This led to an amazing half of a conversation one day. All I heard was the inspector, MH, at the depot saying "Sorry. Can you repeat that? It sounded like a wheel has fallen off your bus...... What do you mean a wheel has fallen off your bus...... What do you mean you can't find it?" It transpired that one of the open top buses was going to the Top of Beachy Head and as it went round a sharp U bend near the top, the driver thought he felt the bus wobble a bit. When he straightened up it seemed OK again so he carried on. It wobbled again so he braked and his offside rear wheel overtook him! It then mounted a small verge on the nearside and disappeared down a slope on the South Downs into some bushes. Some council workers found it a few months later when they were cutting back some vegetation.

In 1976, *The Eastbourne Gazette* was running a campaign calling for reduction in local Government spending and one of its targets was the proposed new bus depot. The editor of the paper was invited to Churchdale Road to see first-hand the problems being faced trying to service longer buses with rear engines in a depot not designed for them. The following week another article appeared in the paper where they apologised and agreed that a new depot was urgently needed. The council, who had earmarked a new site on allotments at the end of Churchdale Road changed their minds and opted for a site on a new trading estate at Birch Road.

There was a warehouse that would form the basis of a depot but did not contain any pits, but there was space on one side where a workshop with eight pits could be built. Like all local government projects, the costs spiralled and the projected cost was increased from £800,000 to over £1m. This did not include another £10,000 for a larger fuel tank. It was 1980 before the project was finished.

There was also no office accommodation, but space for a block to be built. This was agreed to and a two storey office block was erected seemingly as cheaply as possible. This was basically four straight walls using large building blocks that soon acquired the nickname "Lego Lodge". The £247,000 to finance this block was taken from the money put aside to buy new buses.

The workshops moved first with the crews moving there a while later. Sadly the old depot fell into disrepair before finally being demolished and a small housing estate now occupies the site. Moving the operation out of town has the advantage of enjoying more space and paying less council tax, or rates as it was then, but has the disadvantage that it was nowhere near the majority of bus routes so a small fleet of four Ford Fiestas was needed for crew changeovers. These were diesel powered and very nippy. Being used and abused by over 100 different drivers they had a very hard life getting through an awful lot of front tyres as the wheels were spun most times they pulled away.

One of the mechanics acquired a go-cart and kept it hidden in the pits. In the evenings when management had gone home, it was brought out and we would race around the yard in it, making sure no buses could enter by placing a "lookout" man on the entrance gate.

Part of the workshops was taken up by an MOT bay. The bus depot was seen as a fair place to get an MOT done as they were not allowed to fix vehicles that failed, so a fair unbiased test was always assured. Whilst at Churchdale Road, one of the testers was operating a lucrative scam though. This was in the days before computerisation and MOT certificates were just written out from books of numbered certificates. This particular tester kept a book separately for his own purposes and if a motorist approached him directly, rather than book through the office, he would tell them to come back at 5 o'clock when management had gone home. He would then give the vehicle a proper test but pocket the money. His scam only came to light when a motorist, who had been given one of his own certificates, lost it and went down to the offices to apply for a duplicate.

Needless to say, the tester lost his job. Before he did though, he tested an old NSU Quickly moped for me. I had no intention of using the moped, but I wanted to sell the number plate separately and to transfer plates, it required an MOT. The problem was that the brakes were somewhere between pretty poor and non-existent.

Two Northampton Dodge minibuses were used very briefly on loan in the autumn of 1989. No.108 is seen in Cornfield Road at the War Memorial stop on 24th November. (Alan Snatt)

The brake testing procedure was somewhat antiquated though. A sling was passed through the front wheel and this was attached to a large sort of spring balance on the depot wall. The rider would sit on the moped and apply the brakes while the tester would turn a handle that tried to drag the moped towards the wall with the spring balance registering the resistance. I sat astride the moped and dug my heels into the concrete floor pulling on the handlebars as hard as I could while the tester wound the handle. He suspected what I was doing and asked if I was trying to hold it back. I tried smiling through gritted teeth while saying "No". It passed. I never used it on the road again but did manage to sell the number plate.

After the move to Birch Road another MOT bay was added but there was never enough work to keep two bays fully occupied. If idle, the tester was never used for other work, so used to fix drivers' cars in the time between MOTs. He also used to do "pre-MOTs" for us, where we were awarded certificates if they passed and we were not charged if they "failed". This again was in the days prior to computerisation of the system.

At the end of 1986 four Dodge minibuses with East Lancs coachwork were bought to operate a new "Red Carpet" service which served estates where larger buses could not reach. This service was not successful and all four minibuses were sold to Ipswich Buses the following year.

I had built a trike – or more correctly finished one that an Irish chap had started before deciding to return home. The welding had all been finished and it had been sprayed. All I had to do was the wiring, braking system and some finishing touches, one of which was a stereo cassette player. It was a marriage between the back of a Fiat 126 and the front of a Honda 500, not the most 'macho' of trikes you've ever seen. Registering a new vehicle in the 1970s/80s was relatively easy. An MOT was required using the chassis number and having successfully acquired this, a visit to the local Department of Transport in Brighton was needed where presentation of an MOT certificate and road fund licence money resulted in a V5 registration document being issued. I booked in Fifi The Fiat, as I had christened the trike, for an MOT without telling Ray, the tester, it was a trike. I drove into his workshop with "Leader of the Pack" blaring from the stereo. His face was a picture! But he passed it.

When Stagecoach took over, one of the first things they did was close the MOT station.

In 1988, Boroline, who used to be Maidstone Corporation before deregulation in 1986, tendered for some routes in South East London and were successful. These routes were being run by Bexleybus and Boroline expected them to lay off some drivers that they would then re-employ. Unfortunately for them, no drivers were laid off and they found themselves desperate for drivers and they asked other bus companies in the South East, including Eastbourne Buses, if they could help out. Myself and two other drivers volunteered. Very early on a Monday morning we were picked up by a Boroline driver and taken to their depot at Crayford that was being shared with the council's dustcarts. The whole operation was being run from one office in a council building. There was a husband and wife working there who had a young baby. One worked early turns while their spouse worked lates. Their duties overlapped by about 20 minutes so the baby was left in its carrycot in the corridor before being taken home again.

The car we were picked up in used to be the official car of the Mayor of Maidstone and was a stretched Ford Granada limousine; it still had a glass partition between chauffeur and passengers, but had definitely seen better days. Amongst many minor problems with it, two stand out in my mind. The first was that the bonnet would not shut properly and when any speed was reached, air pressure did its best to lift the bonnet causing it to vibrate and bang noisily. Hammering round the M25 early in the morning was a hair-raising, and nearly bonnet raising, experience. The other problem was that the ignition was very worn and the key was on a ring with a host of other keys. The weight of the bunch would pull the key from the ignition. The engine would keep going and it just meant that when one's destination was reached, the keys had to be retrieved from the floor of the car and the correct one found to turn the engine off. We were offered accommodation in the area for the week but declined in favour of commuting using the limo. It was used to get crews between the depot and their buses, so we had to wait until they had finished with it for the day before we could return home, by which time it was dark. We took it in turn to drive. One evening DG was driving and he took a wrong turn in Crayford town centre. NG and I, lounging in the spacious rear seat, were shouting at him to do a U turn. He eventually tried doing one, but in his haste, he stalled it only to discover that the keys had fallen from the ignition again. The interior light did not work so he had to find the correct key from the large bunch in the dark before we could get going again. Needless to say drivers of cars coming at us from both directions were not amused.

No.92 was a Leyland Leopard with Alexander bodywork new to Lancaster City Council in 1976. It was sold to Eastbourne in January 1983 who kept it until December 1988 when it was sold back to Lancaster. (Geoff Morant)

In September 1986 Eastbourne Buses acquired a 1975 Leyland Leopard with Duple Dominant Express coachwork from a local coach company, Vernons, together with the route they operated to Rushlake Green. It was sold to Ensigns of Purfleet in March 1990.

Working there for the week was weird. We were all just shown one route and kept to it all week. Although we had learnt the route, we had no idea of the surrounding area, so when passengers boarded asking for a road that wasn't mentioned on the fare chart, this did lead to problems. Passengers quite rightly expect their drivers to have a certain amount of local knowledge and when they ask for "the butchers" or "the chemist" can't understand why the driver has no idea where they want. I used to show them the fare chart and ask them to pick out the nearest stage and then, more often than not, ask them "Where are we now?"

We were asked to come back for a second week, but we were needed back in Eastbourne, so a week is all we worked there. I wasn't that sorry not to go back, because although we earned good money as we were paid travelling time, they were very long days and I was shattered by the time I finally got home by train on Saturday night.

Back in Eastbourne, one day while loading passengers in the town centre I heard a lady in the queue shout "He's just stolen your purse". The old lady in front of her looked very distressed. Looking in my mirror I saw a youth making off across the road. I leapt from my cab and ran after him. He noticed me and as I caught him up and he threw the purse on to the ground shouting "Take it, take it". I looked at the purse, and then looked at him. I did not want him to get away but I did not want to pursue him any further in case somebody took the purse. Purse? Thief? Purse? Thief? What to do. Before I knew what I had done, I had punched him on the nose! I had never in my life hit anyone before, or since, I hasten to add. I let him run off and I picked the purse up and returned it to the grateful owner. There had been a spate of thefts. The thief would stand at the front of the queue as if he was waiting to board, but in reality he was just looking to see if there were any purses laying on top of bags that could be easily taken. The culprit was never caught, which from my point of view was probably just as well as I could have been prosecuted for assault.

Another occasion when my impetuosity got the better of me was while operating a school trip. The kids were being particularly noisy and rowdy with pupils running around or fighting. Towards the end of the trip, a female pupil was waiting to get off and she looked like a decent young girl and I said to her "Don't you get fed up with having to travel like this?" She replied "Nay. It's alright innit?" and spat

In 1980 Eastbourne Buses ventured into coaching and private hire work with the purchase of two 1976 Leyland Leopards from National Travel East. They were kept for nine years before being sold to Circle Line of Gloucester.

her chewing gum at me. I didn't see why she should get away with this, so I picked up her chewing gum, chased her down the road and saying "I believe this is yours", put it in her long hair. By the time I had returned to the depot her mother had been on the phone and reported me. I was accosted by an Inspector who had the written report in his hand. I told him I was not prepared to put up with this and grabbed the report from his hand making a mental note of the complainant's telephone number. When I arrived home, I phoned the number and spoke to her mother who was not happy. She said her daughter was in tears as she had to have a chunk of her hair cut off. I told her that if her daughter refrained from spitting at other people, it probably wouldn't happen again. She didn't seem to be able to grasp that point. She phoned the depot again to report me for phoning her. The following day I was seen by the Deputy Chief Inspector, RW, who said that I must promise not to phone members of the public like that again. I refused as I told him that I did not make promises I couldn't keep. "But you must", he re-iterated. Again I refused and told him that if in the future I did, we'd have to cross that bridge when we came to it and left it like that.

In the late 1990s, Eastbourne Buses purchased three new DAF coaches with Ikarus bodies for their private hire division. 101 was photographed behind a sister vehicle in Brighton. They were later renumbered 901 onwards.

It did happen again! Soon after the old larger 50p pieces were no longer legal tender, a schoolgirl tendered her fare with one. I gave it back and she told me her mother had given it to her in the morning. "No problem" I said as she gave me a newer version. I thought no more of it. When I returned to the depot I was told her father had phoned accusing me of palming the 50p piece. How dare he? He had never even seen the coin. Anyone knows that if working a school bus, the drivers' priority is to get them all on and off as soon as possible and not hold up the queue by arguing. Again I noted the number on the complaint form and called him. He demanded to know how I got the number. I never told him. I think it's extremely unfair that the public can phone in with completely fabricated stories safe in the knowledge drivers have no comeback.

Another occasion I had a run in with pupils was the last day of term at Willingdon School. This was during the days when all of the services were being one manned and the only crew bus was PD2 No.82 which was only used in emergencies. This particular day, there had been a spate of breakdowns and 82 was the only available bus. I was assigned a relatively new female employee as a clippie. We arrived at the school and I got out of the cab and went round the back for a chat. A group of pupils approached the bus and they had been celebrating the last day of term with a flour fight. I told them in no uncertain terms that this bus was needed for another school run immediately after this one and they would be clearing up any mess they made. I told the clippie who was slightly the nervous type to give me a quick succession of rings on the bell if she had any problems. After about 10 minutes and approaching Stone Cross on our way to Pevensey Bay I heard a "Ding Ding Ding Ding" on the bell. I checked my interior mirror and there was no sign of my clippie. I had no periscope to check the top deck, so I stopped and went to see what the problem was. There was flour all over the top deck. Being a man of my word, I told the clippie to stand on the platform and not let anybody off. I then went off route and returned the bus to the depot. As I was walking across the yard, I passed the Workshop Manager who asked what I was doing. I told him, but he wasn't interested and just walked off. I found a bucket and a mop, took it upstairs and told them we were not going anywhere until it was clean. After a bit of initial resistance, they got to work and cleaned it up and we continued on our way about 15 minutes late. However one of the girls' fathers reported me to the police for kidnapping his daughter. The police did visit the depot but I was not there. They never returned probably because someone took the sensible decision that the caller was wasting police time.

This was the official handover of 12 new Leyland Olympians purchased in 1988. They were the first buses to be delivered in the new biscuit and blue livery.

On circular service 11 is Leyland Olympian No.50. These buses were fitted with fire extinguishers in the cabs that were linked directly to the engine compartment – a very good idea that seems to have been discontinued – not a good decision especially as engine fires seem to be more common. Fuel is now injected into engines under high pressure and any rupture to a fuel line means diesel is sprayed over a hot engine.

Sporting another variation to the biscuit and blue livery on the previous image is another Leyland Olympian leaving the Town Centre with a very light load.

I don't think that management or schools take student behaviour on buses seriously enough. If a pupil is taken to school in a car they have to be sitting down and strapped in while on a bus there can be up to forty standing up. Any scream or shout distracts the driver and all the time they are checking their interior mirror, they are not looking where they are going. There was a school bus in the West Country (Devon I think) that had a fatal accident. Two boys were mucking about and knocked the driver's arm. The bus swerved and hit a tree killing an innocent boy in the top deck front nearside seat. The pupils from the school made a video on how accidents like this happen. I acquired some of these videos and sent them to schools in Eastbourne, but I don't know if any of the schools played them to their students.

One incident that I was not directly involved in but feel it is worth relating involved CT who was driving from Pevensey Bay towards Pevensey one morning. As he approached the level crossing he heard bells ringing although the lights were not flashing. He was too close to the barriers to stop in time but they came down as he crossed the railway line trapping the bus. The level crossing is not manned but operated from Pevensey and Westham signal box about two miles away. The crossing is monitored by CCTV cameras though and luckily the signalman saw the bus, stopped the trains and raised the barriers releasing the bus. The driver was recalled to the depot following such a serious incident and the CCTV from the bus reviewed. When this was played back the flashing lights were clearly visible. CT, an experienced driver, could not understand it. The shop steward representing him, DH, asked him if he had been wearing sunglasses at the time and he confirmed that he was. The CCTV was played again and with the sunglasses on the red lights were not visible. Moral of story – do not wear cheap sunglasses when driving as they can block out red light!

1981 was the last year that AEC Regent Vs were seen on the roads of Eastbourne. To commemorate their passing, the social club was allowed to take one out on a booze cruise to Rye. Bus 56 was used and drivers took it in turns to have one last go in it on the way to Rye but by that time I didn't drink much anyway so stayed sober and drove it back again.

No.16 was the first of a batch of DAF Ikarus single deckers purchased by Eastbourne Buses in February 1994. It was delivered in plain white and given the biscuit and blue livery in our own paint shops before receiving this all over advert promoting the new 12 card tickets.

The following year 1983, the finances of the undertaking were still deteriorating, so the Council paid a firm of consultants, Colin Buchanan and Partners, £30,000 to advise on the best way forward. This company was viewed with some suspicion by the workforce as they had already completed three studies on other South Coast towns, Plymouth, Southampton and Portsmouth and came up with the same solution of cutting routes and increasing fares. Parts of Portsmouth had been left with no service and too many staff were laid off resulting in fewer buses and longer queues. Many staff had to be re-employed and the result was that no savings were made. In Eastbourne, passengers would be interviewed at their homes, work and schools to try to ascertain what they wanted. Call me cynical but I would imagine that the vast majority of passengers would want a bus from outside their house to exactly where they wanted to go with a bus every 5 minutes at half the cost. No-one would push for a worse service and the higher fares that had been recommended elsewhere. What were our management getting paid for anyway? Weren't they supposed to be experts? The study was expected to last six months.

When the report was published, it was much as expected. They found that passengers in this town took longer than average to board. Not really surprising with the aged population. They also found that 37% of those interviewed thought that the crews were rude and unhelpful. They also used a lot of what we saw as "flowery" language in their report. A "slight disbenefit" actually meant a cut of 50%. Recommendations were made that the service should become 100% one man operated and 16 drivers and all the conductors would lose their jobs. They also recommended that more second hand buses be purchased. This led to letters in the local paper proclaiming "Second hand buses for a second class service". The union fought the cuts and I met with a local councillor at his house and pointed out many of the mistakes and fallacies within the report. One was that pensioners who bought a weekly season ticket for £6 only used them on average 6 times each week. As a single fare was only 60p it meant they were losing £2.40. It seemed to open his eyes to their inadequacy. In the event, after a long council meeting it was decided not to implement all of the cuts, but amazingly it was also decided to set up a steering committee to study the plan in detail and pay Buchanans another £12,000 to help implement the parts they were in favour of. The new service started in March and chaos reigned. Nobody knew where the buses were going, despite £1,800 having been spent on publicity, and relief buses had to be put on to cope with demand.

Most of Buchanan's ideas were abandoned during the summer and eventually one councillor apologised and stated that they had "failed miserably". Both the manager, DS, and his Deputy, GL, applied for early retirement, although it was not clear if it was anything to do with the implementation of the report.

In March 1984, a new manager, RB, was engaged. Roger was a very religious man and quietly spoken. The staff thought highly of him because he found time to speak to them and quite often ate in the canteen. He was very smartly dressed and appearances were high on his list of priorities. It was unsurprising therefore that he was against the primrose and brown livery favoured by Buchanan. By September he had come up with four proposed new liveries and buses were parked in the town centre to gauge the public's opinion – see photo at start of this chapter (page 52). A biscuit/blue version of the blue/cream was chosen with the primrose/brown beaten into last place.

No.32 was a 1995 DAF with Northern Counties Paladin body bought in 1997 from Arriva. No.34 was bought at the same time and in 2002 three more, 25/6/7, were purchased.

No.269, formerly No.41, was a DAF with Northern Counties bodywork purchased new in October 1994. The fleet was renumbered for insurance purposes, we were told, with double deckers being numbered 2xx and singles 1xx.

RB was keen on good industrial relations and appointed three staff advisors to the Board. I represented the platform staff, while the other two represented the workshop staff and the inspectors/office staff. We attended board meetings but did not have a vote and there were times when "confidential" items were discussed and we had to leave.

At the end of the year, privatisation of bus services looked to be on the horizon again and RB with the Chairman of the Highways Dept. came up with a cunning plan. This was to ban buses from the town centre and replace them with trolleybuses. This would ensure no competitors could operate in the town. They visited the Commercial Motor Show in Birmingham where a trolleybus chassis designed by GEC and Dennis was on show. Although cleaner for the environment, vehicles would be more expensive to buy and the entire fleet would have to be replaced. The infrastructure cost would also be very expensive. Needless to say the scheme came to nothing but at least they both had an all-expenses paid day out at the Motor Show.

In 1985, the depot was visited by Nicholas Ridley, Secretary of State for Transport who spoke to management and staff about his proposals to deregulate bus services. Councils would still be able to subsidise loss making services but these would have to be awarded to the company that offered best value for money. Staff were not convinced and together with a contingent of local taxi drivers, some of the staff joined a mass rally in London to demonstrate against his proposals. Under his Bill, councils would not be able to own and run their own buses. To circumvent this to a certain extent, Eastbourne Buses Ltd was formed with the shares owned by Eastbourne Borough Council. The Board of the new company would be made up from two working directors and four non-executive directors who were local councillors – 2 Conservative and 2 Liberal. One of the changes that would affect us was that, as we were all part of the East Sussex County Council final salary pension scheme, we would no longer be eligible to stay in it. The Union threatened industrial action and the Council backed down and we were allowed to stay within the scheme.

RB introduced a new service in the town marketed as the "Red Carpet Service" and comprised four ugly looking Dodge minibuses to serve areas of the town that buses couldn't reach. To re-inforce the "Red Carpet" service, the drivers were picked from volunteers and were expected to look smart. These minibuses picked up passengers near their houses and were charged slightly more for the privilege. The service did not get off to a flying start when they all ran out of diesel about 1600 because their fuel tanks were not large enough. Their runnings had to be hastily altered so they could return to the depot to refuel.

The Transport Act became law in October. This had the positive effect that we could bid for Council contracts outside Eastbourne and we were soon running to Uckfield via Hailsham. We could now also finally run to the Top of Beachy Head. The downside was that other operators could compete with us within the town and Southdown bought a fleet of minibuses and started serving Hamlands Estate.

In 1987, RB, not content with running a bus service in Eastbourne was instrumental in setting up Topline, which was to run an operation in Hastings. He had persuaded Southdown and Brighton & Hove to become partners in this new venture, but Brighton & Hove pulled out before the services started leaving Southdown with 51% and Eastbourne Buses with 49%. There was a case to run buses in Hastings as the bus service in the town was becoming dire but it did mean taking the risk of retaliatory action being taken leading to an even worse trading position in Eastbourne. A lot of Eastbourne's better buses were transferred to the new company which led to many complaints from local passengers. These buses were painted in a striking black/yellow livery. Initially the fleet was stabled in Eastbourne but running dead to/from Hastings was time consuming and expensive so a stabling point was soon found at Hastings. This saved £720 each week in diesel and the crews travelled to Hastings together in one bus. Eventually the crews clocked on in Hastings.

1988 saw RB leave to join Stagecoach in London. Before he left he had taken delivery of 12 Leyland Olympians on lease purchase. RB arranged a formal handover of these vehicles and all twelve were lined up in a broad arc outside the workshops. Inside a spread was laid on for the representatives of Leyland, East Lancs bodybuilders and councillors. After the official photos outside the attendees went inside. These buses had already been out in service though and a couple of days before this handover, one had been hit in the rear by a lorry and suffered substantial damage. This bus was unfortunately parked directly outside a window behind the spread, so nobody could miss it.

Twelve DAF Optare Spectras were purchased in 1998. These were Nos 70-81.

DH was appointed as the next MD. I liked David. He was very down to earth and said exactly what he thought. He was very different to RB.

I used to write poems about the bus company and members of staff that were a little near the knuckle sometimes. At Christmas I penned an A-Z of Eastbourne Buses and the verse for H was

H is for Howard
He's the boss and its plain
'Cos he models himself
On Saddam Hussein.

He took it in good humour and when he saw me he said he thought the content was good but the typing was rubbish. I retorted that it shouldn't have been because I got his secretary to type it for me. He smiled, gave me a two-fingered salute and walked away.

He did not always see eye to eye with the non-executive Board members, because he thought the concern should be run more as a business, whereas the councillors on the Board had one eye on the next local elections. He also did away with staff advisers to the Board arguing that only those that had a legal responsibility should be able to make decisions.

The probability that Hastings & District would not take our intrusion into their territory lying down became a certainty when they retaliated in 1985. A fleet of blue and yellow minibuses invaded Eastbourne operating under the name of Eastbourne & District. They ran over our busiest route between Shinewater and Hamlands. The passenger doors to these minibuses were very narrow making it difficult for passengers to board or alight. They were built by Mercedes and, being derived from vans, were not up to the rigours of bus work starting and stopping about every 100yds so became unreliable. However they did take some much needed revenue away from Eastbourne Buses.

Topline made a loss of £338,000 in its first two years of operation and Eastbourne Buses sold its share to Southdown for a nominal amount and it soon merged with H&D.

Hastings & District was owned by Formia which was a company set up by three senior managers. In 1990 they were taken over by Stagecoach, although for a while the acquisition was being investigated by the Monopolies & Mergers Commission. Topline also became part of Stagecoach at about the same time. This would have a bearing on Eastbourne Buses in the future.

1991 saw finances still being a problem and a decision was taken to buy single rather than double deckers to save money and also to lease purchase them rather than buy them outright. Four Javelins were purchased – two new and two fairly new.

In 2002 six of our Optare Spectras were swapped for 10 of Reading's Optare Excels. On the face of it, it may have been a good way of acquiring four extra buses but these turned out to be very unreliable and it was very rare to have more than six on the road at any one time. No.38 was seen in Terminus Road still in Reading livery.

DH informed the Board that Stagecoach had been acting aggressively towards Eastbourne and were still running minibuses from Shinewater. He also informed the Board that if they encroached any further, he would retaliate. In the event, Eastbourne Buses were approached by the MD of Southdown to see if they could work together with a view to reducing competition. One measure was for us to maintain their fleet. Inter-availability of tickets was also proposed.

DH was also a keen transport enthusiast covering railways and trams, as well as buses. One day a low-loader arrived at the depot carrying the diesel locomotive from the Romney, Hythe & District Railway. Tracks were laid into the paint shop and it was off-loaded. When it emerged again, it was in Eastbourne Buses livery.

At the same time DH was being taught how to drive a steam engine at the RH&DR. A new service was introduced that started in Eastbourne and wound its way through the villages of Bodiam and Northiam finishing at New Romney Station. The whole journey took all day and was a welcome relief from driving round the streets of Eastbourne. One can only speculate what deal had been done!

One morning during the run out, one of the drivers, MH, who was driving a Dennis Dart, drove down one of the lanes and smashed into the old AEC Regal that was parked outside the workshops. The accident caused extensive damage. The reason for the accident was never fully established. Mick maintained the bus suffered from a power surge and just took off. Many, including management, were sceptical with this explanation. There were stories that he was drinking a cup of coffee or standing up changing the blinds and he pressed the accelerator rather than the brake. His explanation of a power surge was not that unbelievable because other Darts had been reported suffering the same problem. In 1992 there were 13 cases reported of power surges, six of which included collisions. In 1998 another Dart careered into passengers at Sunderland Bus Station killing two. The driver was found not guilty after his council argued that engineering tolerances on Darts meant that the accelerator in some buses was sometimes higher than the brake pedal.

No.43, an ex-Reading Excel, now with an all over advert for the local Vauxhall dealership. The buses acquired from Reading had all been new to Cardiff Buses in 1997.

Mick was disciplined, but not sacked, probably because he had worked for the company for many years. Instead he was found a job as an MOT assistant. Many of us joked at the time that management thought it was better for him to be driving other people's vehicles rather than our own. The Regal was in fact an economic write-off, but somehow DH found the resources to restore it to its former glory.

In 1994, the Board asked DH to look into the viability of running a bus that linked the Cross-Channel ferry at Newhaven with Eastbourne. This is an example of where councillors are not too savvy when it comes to running a business. DH reported back that there were 4 sailings each day averaging less than 100 foot passengers per sailing. A train already met the ferry. It was also pointed out that a service would also have to operate to a timetable and if the ferry was late, the bus could not wait, thereby defeating the object. The idea was dropped.

1999 saw a Liberal councillor trying to make political capital from the bus service complaining "We haven't got a bus service in Eastbourne. It's as simple as that." The Liberal councillors on the Board disagreed with him as did many correspondents, (including myself), in the local press. I pointed out that it was in his party's hands to improve off peak services by putting them out to tender. He never responded to the criticisms.

The AGM that year did not go according to plan. Just after it had started, the Leader of The Council, Bert Leggett and Eastbourne's Chief Executive, Sari Conway, entered the meeting and stopped the proceedings. They informed the Board Members that they had been having secret talks with the French firm of Cariane in order to sell off some of the shares. They then made all those present sign deeds of confidentiality.

Rumours around the depot were rife. The union wrote to the Council to seek assurances that our jobs were safe. We also thought that the public should be aware that their bus service could be sold. We could not risk putting our names to a letter to the press, so my partner, who lived in Seaford, volunteered.

A Steering Committee was set up to discuss the sale of the shares. This consisted of leaders and deputy leaders of the local Liberal and Conservative parties, top council officials and two trade union reps, including myself. We convened in a meeting room at the Town Hall. SC chaired the meeting and started by saying that there had been a serious breach of confidentiality and produced the very letter that my partner had sent to the Eastbourne Herald. Not a copy of it, but the actual letter. She went on to say that although the contents were not 100% accurate, it was obviously written by somebody fairly well

2002 saw the purchase of six Wright bodied DAFs. They seemed to have complicated electrics and there was a slight delay on everything working – including the horn!!

Painted in gold to celebrate Her Majesty's Golden Jubilee in 2002 was DAF No.55 in Princes Road.

Another bus to be repainted to celebrate an event was DAF No.53 painted in Eastbourne Bus's blue/yellow livery to mark their 110th anniversary.

informed. It had been rumoured that SC had a very good relationship with the editor and this seemed to bear that out.

One councillor asked if the person who wrote the letter existed or if it had been written using a false name. My heart was in my mouth. She replied that she was real and that they would be contacting her to find out where she got the information from. I could feel the sweat forming on my brow. After a few more questions and suggestions a senior Tory councillor said "I know how we can find out who wrote it. We'll find out who she's sleeping with!" I swallowed hard - very hard, but luckily nobody noticed.

The meeting continued without being me found out. My union colleague, IS, and I were both asked to sign the same confidentiality document as the rest of the committee, but we refused on the grounds that it was our duty to inform our membership of the ongoing situation. In the end we agreed that, for financially sensitive items on the agenda, we would leave the meeting.

I put up posters on bus shelters informing passengers of the proposed sell out and urged them to contact their local councillors. DH turned a blind eye to this as he too was against the sale.

A couple of days after the Town Hall meeting, the postman delivered a large plain brown envelope. Inside were a number of posters claiming all sorts of derogatory statements about serving council officials and councillors. I think the anonymous sender expected me to post these round the town as well. However I took them into the depot to show the management. They already had a copy which had been faxed from the Town Hall and I was informed that a policeman was on his way to interview me. Luckily the original had been faxed to the Town Hall from a business within Eastbourne Station and he had been caught on CCTV. The policeman when he arrived, realised that I was not involved but the culprit was an ex-employee that both management and myself recognised, so he was visited by the law. My innocence was not accepted by SC and I was thrown off the steering committee. At the time, the Deputy Leader of the Liberals was Gary Potter, an old drinking buddy of mine. I phoned him about the situation but he would not return my calls. I bumped into him a while later and he told me he had been advised by the Chief Executive's office not to speak to me.

Sari Conway was eventually sacked by the council for the way she had been treating staff. She offered her resignation just before the council meeting that decided her fate, but her offer was rejected and she was dismissed without notice. She retired to Rye where she ran a fish and chip shop.

DH unexpectedly handed in his notice in August. This came as a shock to the staff, but we understood his reasons as we thought he had been treated diabolically by the council. He was to take up a post where he was in charge of all the public transport on The Isle of Man, where his newly learnt steam engine driving skills came in very handy.

It was decided not to replace him until the sale of shares had been finalised and the Financial Director, AC, was temporarily put in charge

SB was eventually appointed the new MD. AC was made redundant and an accountant, KD, employed, but he was eventually also made a Director. SB had come from Stagecoach and although we didn't realise it immediately, unfortunately he brought Stagecoach ways with him.

The outcome of the negotiations was that 20% of the company was sold to Cariane for £462,000, which entitled them to one seat on the Board. They had put forward a radical restructuring of the routes in the town. I have not seen the report, but the strictly confidential response to it recently came into my hands and the French scheme was shown up to be totally unworkable. This is not just my view, but the view of Eastbourne Buses Directors, Management and the Council's own Transport Consultant. It is too long to go into detail here but to give you a flavour of their ideas (and apologies to readers who do not know Eastbourne) it was proposed to pull out of one end of Larkspur Drive and instead buses would go down Milfoil Drive, turn left into Larkspur Drive as far as Rotherfield Avenue, reversing into the aforementioned and returning by the same route. Other roads that they proposed would lose their services were Green Street, Sevenoaks Road, The Rising and Lewes Road. They proposed sending some buses along some roads that are totally unsuitable e.g. Royal Sussex Crescent and Colwood Crescent. Another idea was to run through from North to South Harbours even though there is not a direct road linking the two and council had no intention of building one. They also proposed cutting the links over Hampden Park level crossing. This part of their plan was implemented until

Eastbourne Buses tried route branding some of their buses by painting a broad stripe along the bottom of the bodywork. The green stripe seen here was supposed to denote "country services". It later had "The South Downs Connection" printed above the windscreen which seemed strange to me as it was used on the Tunbridge Wells run which is away from the South Downs.

Another bus with route branding although nobody knew what it stood for was No.33. It was one of two 1998 Dennis Darts with Marshall Capital bodies that had been new to Travel de Courcey of Coventry and purchased by Eastbourne Buses in April 2006.

numerous complaints had it reinstated. Another non-starter was a route that ran in the evenings that left the town Centre, served Bridgemere, most of the estates in Langney and Lottbridge Drove before returning to the town. Two buses per hour were envisaged but the service only went one way. There was no returning service!

Why do some people/companies who have never visited the town think they can devise a better service than one that has evolved over 100 years to serve the changing needs of the population? And why do those in power in the town have so little faith in those managers they have employed for many years?

They also advised swapping some of our doubles for single deckers even though cancelling the leases on the doubles would be very costly. In the event 6 of our Optare Spectras were swapped for 10 of Reading's single deck Excels. They had only had them for 12 months, having acquired them from Cardiff. This may have seemed reasonable on the face of it, but these Excels proved to be very unreliable – one even broke down while being delivered. Reading were probably only too pleased to see the back of them. SB came under a lot of criticism for this deal, but how much pressure he was under to do the deal is not known.

When the operations manager resigned, SB employed JB, who was also ex-Stagecoach. The number of disciplinaries shot through the roof. No longer was there a quiet word in your ear if you had done wrong. Everything was done in a formal manner. Morale was beginning to slip. It was alleged JB also had a drink problem. I was defending a driver one morning over a trivial matter and JB's hand was shaking so much, he could not write. I asked him if he wished to adjourn the meeting but he declined.

One of the things the new regime was very keen on was the compulsory wearing of ties. The fleet was deteriorating with most of the buses having accident damage or panels painted a different shade, but I thought they were putting too much emphasis on the crews looking smart, when the vehicles were far from it. Uniform regulations were eased during the summer months when a tie need not be worn but if a jumper or jacket was worn, then a tie had to be put on. I jokingly told one of the shop stewards that I was thinking of converting to the Muslim religion as they regarded a tie as a form of the cross and thereby a Christian symbol. Unknown to me he relayed this to management and they took it seriously! They even sent me a report with the name of a Muslim cleric that preached that the wearing of a tie was acceptable. Oh dear!

Soon after that conversation, I took over a bus on route 13, one of the circular routes. A minibus was on this running, which was totally unsuitable for this busy route but had been the only available vehicle. I had not gone far when a replacement vehicle that had just come straight from the workshop was bought out to me.

I transferred my passengers and carried on. I had not gone far when I went over a sleeping policeman traffic calming measure and the bus was so low on its suspension that it grounded. I radioed in for a replacement. A DAF single was brought to me. The windscreen on the nearside was very badly cracked from top to bottom. When I arrived at Langney Shopping Centre an elderly lady boarded and complained that I was about 20 minutes late. I apologised but pointed out that I was wearing a tie! She understandably looked a bit dumbfounded at my response. I was working an early turn that day and finished about 3.00. I was debating with myself whether to just go home or put in a report about the state of the fleet. I decided to take the trouble of writing a report, but thought that a degree of sarcasm would make it stand out from other reports. I relayed the afternoon's events including the lady's reaction to my comment on ties. I finished by saying that I was sure that this report would be acted on, but then put "Is that men in white coats I can see getting closer coming to taking me away?". I signed off "May Allah be with you". JB was not in his office so I left it on his desk. A while later I heard him in his office and went back in to tell him that the report should be read in the spirit it had been written. "It has," he said, "You're suspended from duty."

As I was a shop steward, I was entitled to be represented by a full time union official. On the day of the hearing, SW arrived and said she would like a meeting with SB before I went in. When she returned, she said that I had been given a choice. I could either go ahead with the disciplinary hearing (DP) or be sent on a union shop steward's course to learn how to behave properly. Unsurprisingly, I chose the latter and had a week off work to attend the course at union offices in Crawley.

That was not the only run in I had with them over ties. A notice had been put up in the duty room detailing the changes to the uniform agreement and as the union had objected to the changes, we were given 90 days' notice before implementation. I was working a late turn and clocked on not wearing a tie. Another driver who had clocked on just before me complained that he had been told off for being improperly dressed. I went back to the inspector and asked why he had been spoken to and not me. In that case he said "Put your tie on" I refused. He went and found the senior inspector who also told me to put a tie on. Again I refused, so he went to see SB. He came back and told me that the MD had said that I was to put a tie on or go home. Not one to turn down a day off with pay I bid them farewell and told them to read the last paragraph of the staff notice which mentioned 90 days' notice. I had only been home about 10 minutes when the phone rang. I ignored it. It had been the depot inviting me back to work again.

I had always been against rules for the sake of rules and there were a couple of instances when this occurred. We used to have to sign on with our signature, clock number and time. This was fine until the system was computerised and the control inspectors signed us in on a different sheet and if we were late the arrival time was noted and we countersigned it. A much better system, I thought. But they also kept the old system of signing on as well. These sheets of paper were simply filed away at the end of the day. I decided to stop signing on and no-one noticed until a month or two later when a dispute arose about another driver's arrival time and the shop steward told management that I never signed on. When I arrived for a late turn that day, the Inspector told me I had to sign on. I refused stating it was all a waste of time and paper. Management were called and after a discussion lasting about 30 minutes, my shop steward advised me that it was an agreement that I should sign on.

I relented, but used a false signature and wrong clock number. This carried on unnoticed for a few weeks until clocking on one day the same manager saw me signing on and said he was pleased I was still doing it. I told him about the false signature and false clock number. Within two weeks this system had been dispensed with.

There used to be a supply of painkillers kept in case anyone had a headache or other minor ailment. It then became illegal to hand these out without the signature of the person taking them. This was another waste of paper but out of the hands of management, but they supplied an exercise book with columns for date, name, how many taken and ailment. I had a headache one evening so was given the tablets and the book. I thought I'd test the system and entered that I had taken 20 pills in an attempted suicide! I handed the book back and never heard another thing about it. The Health & Safety Brigade have since banned companies from handing out painkillers.

No.36 was a 1990 Dennis Dart with Caetano bodywork.

INTO THE NEW CENTURY

In 2001 there was a scheme put forward to introduce bus lanes in the town. The initial timetable proposed by Cariane a couple of years previously was dependent on these being installed. Council officials, management, another shop steward and I went out in one of the buses to survey where these were needed most. Places we identified included Kings Drive around the Rodmill Roundabout and St. Anthony's Avenue approaching Tescos. One of the officials said the St.Anthony's idea would be a non-starter because some of the houses did not have driveways and if they gave homeowners permission to build one knowing a bus lane was to be installed, they could be sued if they reversed their vehicles out and hit a bus. Unbelievable! No wonder nothing gets done in this country. They decided that the best place to build the first one would be adjacent to Seaside Recreation Ground approaching Whitley Road traffic lights. This decision was based on the presumption there would be less opposition to this as it was not outside any houses. In the event, a few people complained

The logo on the side of this Leyland Olympian was because Eastbourne Buses was celebrating its centenary in 2003. (Mark Lyons)

Showing the frailties of electronic blinds was Cadet No.53 with the middle part of its destination missing. We never had that problem with roller blinds! (Mark Lyons)

and the scheme was delayed...... and delayed....... and delayed.......
and finally scrapped.

2002 saw Eastbourne Buses spend some of the money raised by the sale of 20% of its shares to Cariane. They purchased the routes operated by Stagecoach from their Cavendish Place depot. I never understood why we purchased them. Stagecoach obviously wanted to close their town centre premises so they could be sold for redevelopment. Why then pay for routes that we could have simply registered? One can only surmise. The staff that worked at Cavendish Place were taken on at Eastbourne Buses under TUPE arrangements. The routes taken on were the circular service that linked up Pevensey, Stone Cross and Polegate with the town centre. The longer route to Tunbridge Wells via Hailsham, Heathfield and Mayfield was also obtained. This route is over 50km long so comes under European, rather domestic, driving laws. This means that tachographs had to be used and driving hours are more restricted. For example the longest spell of driving is 4½ hours rather than 5 ½ hours allowed round the town. It also meant that more time must be taken on overnight rests and fewer days can be worked before a rest day must be taken. Why this is so is a mystery to me as driving a return trip to Tunbridge Wells is certainly no harder than four

No.277 in all-over blue livery was another vehicle bought second hand by Eastbourne Buses. It was a Leyland Olympian with Alexander bodywork supplied when new to Armchair of Brentford. (Mark Lyons)

Another route to have branding applied was the 1/1A. Why the main route through the town was branded 'The Cavendish Connection' is beyond me. Intending passengers could see the destination blind long before they could see the stripe down the side, so it seemed a bit pointless. (Mark Lyons)

hours driving around Eastbourne. There again why can a bus driver work for 5½ hours without a break? Lorry drivers have to take a legal break after 4½ hours. Are humans less valuable than 10 tons of sand, for example.

As tachos were needed for this and the East Grinstead service we were also running a separate rota was created just for those on tacho work. I decided to try this rota out and am glad I did. I found that driving to Tunbridge Wells offered a variety of driving challenges from busy towns and quiet villages to fast dual carriages and narrow country lanes. I also found that the passengers in the country were friendlier than those on some Eastbourne estates. Having to fill out a tacho every day was a pain but one worth putting up with.

One of the problems with running a country route is the time it takes for mechanics to reach you in the event of a breakdown especially in the case where the depot is at one extreme end of the route as is the 51 to Tunbridge Wells. Arriva's depot staff have proved helpful in the past letting us top up radiators or jump starting buses with flat batteries although fixing a rival's bus does not come high on their list of priorities. I broke down at the bus stand at Meadow Road in Tunbridge Wells with an air leak. I waited over an hour for one of our mechanics to attend and as soon as he arrived he said he couldn't fix it because the bus was on the public highway and he wasn't allowed to go beneath it. I asked why he had bothered coming out as I had told them where the bus was. He just said I would need a tow back to the depot and would arrange it. I looked forward to this because the towing vehicle would be one of Mick Gould's massive American breakdown trucks. This duly arrived. The driver looked under the bus, identified the problem and couldn't understand why our mechanic didn't fix it. He got to work and attached the bus, lifting the front clear of the road. I jumped into his cab, which was left hand drive, and we set off back to Eastbourne. The A267 out of Tunbridge Wells is a steep hill yet he drove up there faster than I could go in the bus! The power in his truck was unbelievable and an unforgettable experience.

There had been sporadic problems with youths on the Shinewater Estate at Langney. Missiles had been thrown at buses. Engine covers at the rear of buses were pulled up in attempts to lure the driver from his cab. If he fell for it one of the yobs would make an attempt to steal the driver's takings. A variation on this scheme was to put a couple of wheelie bins in the road to stop the bus. One evening while driving round the estate, a driver coming the other way flagged me down and told me I would probably be shot at in Milfoil Drive. I gingerly continued and was beginning to breathe a sigh of relief

Even more confusing was this attempt at branding. Some runnings meant that buses were used on two routes – in this case routes 2 and 3, so the front half was branded differently to the rear! Notice the blind still has not been fixed even though it has been in the workshops for repainting. (Mark Lyons)

when I reached the top of the road when there was a loud crack and a side window shattered. I pulled up round the corner, jumped out and tried to creep up behind any gunman. "What am I doing?" did cross my mind, but at that moment it started raining so I returned to my bus. I didn't mind risking being shot, but I wasn't going to get wet as well. Unbeknown to me an inspector had been driving behind me and noticed a youth at a bedroom window with an air rifle. The police were called and he was arrested. As a "victim" I had a say in his punishment. I thought the punishment should fit the crime so suggested that he should spend a day at the depot cleaning the buses. Management agreed. I was told by Victim Support that this would happen sometime in the next year. Year! As far as I know it never did take place.

I got into the habit of taking a camcorder to work with me to record any events. Late one night a driver radioed in saying he was having problems with two passengers on the same estate. I attended with the inspector and took the camcorder with me. On arrival a teenage boy and girl were off the bus still arguing with the driver. I stayed back a bit and started filming. Suddenly the lad dived onto the bus, grabbed the driver's cash tray and ran off. The police were called and I supplied them with a DVD copy of my evidence. A few days later they contacted me to ask if I had any better images because the culprit was one of identical twins and they could not tell which one was guilty. Under questioning, they blamed each other, so they got away with it. On more than one occasion, evening services have been withdrawn from this estate, but recently the "natives" seem to have got the message and are reasonably well behaved.

There was one occasion where a guy had been getting on buses all day without paying. I think he was homeless and wasn't causing any trouble, and probably just wanted somewhere warm to sit. He had been thrown off three or four times during the course of the day, but then just got on another bus. During the evening, the control inspector, RP, put out a message over the radio that on no account were we to let him on again. About 23.20 on my last trip, I stopped at Langney Shopping Centre and noticed this chap sitting in a corner of the shelter. I thought I'd wind the inspector up, so radioed in saying that he had just got on again. RP was not happy. I wound him up even more by saying I was bringing him back to the depot. It took me about 10 minutes to get to the depot and I was chuckling to

It seems No.54 was suffering with the same problems with its destination blind as No.53. Where it was bound for – well your guess and mine is probably as good as the passenger's! (Mark Lyons)

myself all the way. But as I turned into Birch Road, he was waiting outside the depot for me, and had flagged down a passing police car for assistance. He jumped on the bus and said "Where is he?" I told him I had only been joking, so he had to apologise to the police saying I had managed to get him off. He then vowed to pay me back!

In 2005 Eastbourne Buses took over the operation of the Dotto train. They paid the Council £30,000 to do so and bore all the operating costs but kept any profit made up to £25,000; any profit above that sum would be shared between the bus company and Council. MS applied for, and got, the job of driving one of the two trains. Part of the journey between the harbour in the east and the Foot of Beachy Head ran along the town's wide promenade. On one journey returning from the Foot, he was in collision with an elderly lady who sustained a broken leg. He was taken to court for careless driving even though he claimed the lady walked into the side of the train and he could not avoid the accident. He said that the funnel on

An ailing Eastbourne Buses gambled on leasing 10 MAN singles hoping that the leasing costs would be mainly met by the savings on maintaining their older buses. No.62 is seen in the new two-tone blue livery. (Mark Lyons)

the front of the train obscured his vision. The judge found him guilty because he said that if you drive a vehicle with restricted vision, you are guilty of careless driving even if you don't hit anything. He gave him an absolute discharge though. Chatting with his defence council after the trial I asked if MS would have to tell his insurance company when his policy was due for renewal. He could not give me an answer as he had never known a case where a driver had been found guilty but given an absolute discharge.

Whilst waiting for the outcome of the trial, the Dotto Train had not been running and a lot of much needed income had been lost. After the case JE, another shop steward, and I were approached by RB, who stated that although the Dotto was not scheduled to return to service until after a meeting with the Regional Organiser of the Union, SW, the following Tuesday, he said that the weather forecast for the weekend was really good and he would like to see it back in service straight away. Before it could run again though, the funnels would have to be removed from both trains and warning notices would have to be posted the entire length of the promenade warning pedestrians of the presence of the Dotto train. JE and I printed and laminated the posters and spent the evening attaching them to lamp posts. The Dotto went out and had a very successful weekend.

I was taken off the road on the following Tuesday to attend the meeting but when SW arrived she was inexplicably annoyed with me. She called me "a snake in the grass, a company rat" and other phrases that cannot be repeated here. I don't know why she was so upset with me. She had no quarrel with the other shop steward. She also banned me from attending the meeting with management although she had no right to do so.

I didn't go to the meeting but spent my time making out an official complaint about her to the union hierarchy. I was eventually asked to make an official statement at the union offices at Crawley. JE was also summoned to make a witness statement. I waited to hear the outcome of my complaint. After a few weeks, I had heard nothing so I enquired why it was taking so long and still heard nothing. I contacted the Regional Secretary who ignored me. I reminded him that ignoring people was a form of bullying. He ignored me again. In desperation I opened a website www.uniteourunion.co.uk which was a simple page inviting members to complain about full time officials. I emailed him to tell him what I had done. Sixteen minutes later I got a reply! He was not happy but I did eventually get a written document with the outcome of my complaint but it was heavily redacted. I must say here that our replacement full time officer, DW, was very good.

As stated earlier the ex-Reading Excels were very unreliable and there was nearly always one bus having a new engine or gearbox fitted. One particular mechanic was responsible for replacing these and used to work in a bay away from the main workshops. He had a special hoist onto which the power unit was hung to be moved. One day this toppled over crushing him beneath it. He was lucky inasmuch that a delivery driver was just arriving at the depot soon after the accident had happened and raised the alarm. The mechanic was very badly injured. Not only did he have broken ribs, but more seriously one of his lungs was damaged as was a heart muscle. He was in a coma for four days and had to spend six weeks in hospital, three of which were in intensive care and unfortunately he was unable to work again.

The Health & Safety Executive investigated the accident. They found that the engine and gearbox had been removed from the bus as one unit. It had then been separated and two other mechanics had taken the gearbox away. The mechanic had lain down to replace a hose and it is thought that he was holding on to the engine when he tried to pull himself up. They came to the conclusion that removing the gearbox had made the hoist unstable and his added weight had caused it to topple over. The company was found guilty of failing to carry out a risk assessment on separating the engine whilst on the hoist. They were fined £25,000 with costs of £12,725.

The Health & Safety Executive made subsequent visits to the depot to check on other procedures. As I was a H&S rep at the depot I was invited to join a party of management and an H&S official on a walk round check of the depot. Things were going quite well until the lady from the H&S Executive opened a door in the workshops to reveal a dartboard on the other side. "It's a good thing they weren't playing a game now," she said. The mechanics present assured her that they always locked the door when playing. The pressure was beginning to get to SB and he whispered to me that he was going back to his office to shoot himself, and left the party!

In 2006 DH returned from the Isle of Man and started another bus company in direct competition with Eastbourne Buses. He joined forces with Christian Harmer, a director of Renown Coaches to form Cavendish Motor Services. They ran two routes in the town under the name of The Lighthouse Line and cleverly adopted the livery that Southdown used to use. The two routes were numbered 10 and 11. One crossed the town in an east/west direction and the other served Hailsham via a different route to Eastbourne Buses. They ran strictly on a commercial basis with no early morning, evening or weekend services. This allowed them to undercut the fares we were charging.

Staff relations continued to deteriorate and when the next pay deal was offered the staff turned it down. Many of the "No" votes were placed, not because the offer was unreasonable bearing in mind the finances of the company, but more as a vote of no confidence against the management and the way we were being treated. The dispute escalated and the first of two one-day strikes took place on June 15th 2006. Only just over 50% had voted and only just over 50% of those voted to strike, so we were unsure of how much support there would be on the day. As it turned out, support was very good. Only about 4 or 5 drivers broke the strike. Ironically one of those, who lived on a large estate at Hampden Park, had his front door window smashed. I was called in by management who intimated it was one of the committee that had smashed it. It wasn't. Although it was common knowledge that he intended to work, we would not stoop so low. It was most likely to be a passenger living nearby who was annoyed at there being no service and knew he was a driver, but did not realise he intended working.

2007 saw the purchase of four 1999 DAFs with Alexander bodies. Second hand low floor double deckers were very hard to come by at the time. These had been owned by the Manchester company, UK North, who had had their operating licence revoked due to poor maintenance. They were in a terrible state and it took months before all four were roadworthy and even then they proved to be very unreliable. (Mark Lyons)

The day of the strike was nice and sunny, so as I said earlier support was good. One driver parked his camper van outside the depot and kept us supplied with teas and coffees. When one of the managers arrived for work, I stood in the middle of the drive to block his progress. He drove his car up against my legs and started pushing me with his bumper. A policeman was watching this. I shouted to him that he was trying to run me over. "Get out of the bloody way then" was his response. So I did. The councillors on the Board visited the depot on the day and were shown round by management. Not one of them bothered to come and talk to us, which was a shame as they might have found out the real reason for the strike if they had. The Chairman was a Tory, who always gave the impression of being better than us, so I had to give a wry smile when he was later taken to court for not paying his council tax.

I think the strength of feeling shook the management and constructive talks were held which resulted in the second strike being called off. Relations generally improved after the strike.

One of the drivers, MS, used to wear an earpiece so he could listen to music as he drove round. It is not a practice that I approve of and nor did the company. He was spotted by a road inspector and reported. At his disciplinary, he was given a final warning. A while later whilst in slow moving traffic in Polegate High Street he put it in again. He noticed another road inspector and removed it quickly, but not before he had been spotted. He was disciplined again and sacked. He found a job driving for another local bus company, but appealed his dismissal. In those days, the appeal was heard by the four councillors on the Board, and the MD was not present at the hearing. The appeal was to be heard prior to a Board meeting one evening. I was representing MS but did not hold out much hope, arguing that he was only travelling at about 5mph and therefore not dangerous. We had a new driving instructor, RR. and on the day of the appeal, he entered my office and informed me that he had been employed incognito for the past couple of weeks and had been charged with travelling round on buses reporting on the standards of driving. He handed me four reports on drivers he considered were verging on dangerous and needing further retraining. I could not believe my luck – they were like manna from heaven. At the hearing that evening, I argued the case that the punishment of dismissal was too harsh and at 5mph his actions weren't dangerous and then threw the driving assessments of the four "dangerous" drivers into the middle of the table and said that all drivers must be treated equally and fairly and these four drivers had not been disciplined at all and might even be out on the road as we spoke.

The meeting was adjourned and when we were called back in, MS was reinstated. He telephoned me about 22.30 that night to say that he had just received a call from the depot to say that he was to report for duty the following morning. He said that he was still expected at his other job and didn't know what to do. I told him he would have to apologise to his new boss for letting them down because if he went to work for them the next day, Eastbourne Buses would probably dismiss him for working for a rival company.

A fatal accident took place in the depot at Birch Road on September 4th 2006 when a driver, Roy Trundell, was squashed between two buses. It was a strange series of events that led up to the accident. About 08.45 Roy had just brought a bus into the yard and parked directly behind another one in Lane 9. Another driver, who had been a bit late for work had just got into the bus in front. As he had walked to his bus he had not noticed Roy driving round the yard and at that time the space behind his bus was clear. He had a bus parked immediately in front of his. He started his bus up and reversed up to give him room to drive round the bus in front. He did this at the exact moment that Roy had left his cab and walked between the two vehicles, trapping him.

Some buses had a life after Eastbourne Buses. Ex No.16 is seen in Provincial's livery. It was one of three that were sold to the Gosport and Fareham Company in 1988.

In yet another livery was dual purpose vehicle No. 27, a Dennis Javelin with Plaxton bodywork, unusually seen on service 1. Crews and passengers hated this vehicle because of the steep steps from the road to the saloon which meant a struggle for the passengers and timekeeping problems for the driver. (Alan Snatt)

A couple of things bothered me about this. The duty that Roy was on was worked regularly by him and he knew that the bus he had brought back to the depot was due out straight away, so why did he park it in such an awkward place for the next driver? Also the driver who reversed up would not have had time to start the engine and select reverse gear while Roy was behind the bus so the engine was running when Roy walked between them. He should also have been able to hear the reversing horn. Did Roy believe that because he was wearing a hi-vis jacket that he had been seen? We shall never know. In the 100 years of operation without hi-vis there were no pedestrian accidents within the depot.

In the 44 years I have been driving I have seen many pedestrian accidents and the vast majority of these have been on, or near, zebra and pelican crossings. People think they are safer on a crossing and don't take nearly as much notice of oncoming traffic as they do when crossing elsewhere.

The inquest returned a verdict of accidental death. This accident, of course brought further scrutiny from the H&S Executive and both the company and SB, as an individual, faced charges.

I think that the depot was a safe place to work and the accident, though tragic, was a combination of a set of factors that would never occur again. Again, I was in a party of H&S inspectors and management that did a walk round check at the depot. A number of minor recommendations were made such as another notice on a door or the moving of a Give Way line a couple of feet. What concerned me more was that our rivals at Cavendish Motors were working from a piece of waste land with no overhead lighting, lane markings, one way systems etc. The H&S representatives weren't interested though. They were focused on taking Eastbourne Buses to court. I pursued the matter with the rep asking him if would not be better to try to prevent another accident waiting to happen at a relatively dangerous site than pursue a company that had got its house in order. He said that I should put in an official complaint. When I said I intended to, he agreed to look at the site on his way home.

I also looked on Google Earth at the car park of the H&S offices at Oxted but their car park had no walkways or one way systems and it seemed to be unfair that they were ignoring their own advice.

Eventually SB was fined £5,000 with £5,000 costs and the company £100,000 with £135,000 costs for breach of H&S rules.

The strain had been having an effect on SB's health and he was having long periods off sick. A new summer service had been registered but no duties had been compiled. I had become interested in how duties were compiled during the time DH was in charge and attended a union course on the subject.

In a nutshell, the way duties are compiled is with the use of a large sheet (about 3' x 2'). Longitudinally the sheet is marked out with Hours and vertically with Running Numbers. Each running is then entered on the chart – if Running 1 went out at 06.00 and stayed out on the road until 22.30 then a line is drawn between these two times and any possible changeover times are marked along the line. This is done for all runnings. Compiling can then start. For example Duty 1 would take out Running 1 from 06.00 until 10.00. A pencil line is then drawn between these points and DD1 is written on this line. A 30 minute break is then needed so then another running is sought that can be taken over soon after 10.30 and could work until about 14.00. This is done until all the pieces of work are covered. The process starts off relatively easily but gets harder towards the end as the pieces of work left don't go together to make up an economic duty. That's when other pieces already allocated have to be swapped about and it is very easy for mistakes to be made. It is very satisfying though when the last piece has been allocated.

The Operations Manager at the time, AY, was getting concerned that SB would not return in time to compile the Monday – Friday duties and asked me if I could do so at home and in my time providing I was supplied with the running sheets. I agreed and spent all my spare time over the next week or two in doing so. I ran into trouble compiling these as I had a number of pieces of work of about two hours long all in the early afternoon which I could not fit into any duties and keep them under the maximum length of 9 hours. I eventually solved the problem by putting some on the end of early turns and some on the start of late turns creating 10 hour days that formed a 4 day working week. These duties suit many drivers. The days are long and tiring but it does mean having three rest days every week. Those in need of money also had the opportunity of working three rest days. Management agreed to the creation of separate rotas to accommodate these duties. I was then asked to compile Saturdays which I did. SB had still not returned so I compiled Sundays as well. SB did return just as I finished these duties and I told him I wanted paying £200 for my time compiling these duties. He laughed and refused. I pointed out that I had put a copyright symbol and my name on every sheet and if he posted them on the duty room walls, I would sue him. He relented and we came to an agreement that I would be paid 40 hours overtime. There are now computerised systems that allow different criteria to be imputed and duties are compiled automatically but without the sense of achievement.

We had the feeling there was some friction between AY and the Directors and he eventually left. LP replaced him. He had taken early retirement from a managerial post at the Post Office. He must have been used to starting early in the morning as more often than not he was in his office by 06.00 and sometimes even earlier. I found both these managers good to work with although we did not always see eye to eye.

It was becoming obvious that Eastbourne Buses was in serious financial trouble. Some suppliers had stopped trading with us and SB confided in me that the fuel companies were paid a month in arrears and after two more tanker loads had been delivered and if they demanded money up front, that would be the final nail in our coffin. A tanker holds about 30,000 litres so two tanker loads were worth about £25,000 at the time. Fuel prices were rising dramatically at the time, as were insurance costs. I was told that insurance was costing nearly £1,000 each day! Many staff blamed SB for the financial state of the company. They may have been correct to a certain extent but were unaware of the many factors outside of his control.

I did not realise at the time that as soon as a bus was paid for it was re-mortgaged. The cost of keeping these old buses on the road was becoming very expensive, so the decision was taken to lease some MANs. It was hoped that the increase cost in leasing these would be met by the savings in maintaining the older, less reliable, vehicles. The Excels were sold to South Gloucester Bus and Coach owned by Rotala. Two mechanics travelled with the convoy in case of breakdowns but remarkably they all made the journey without incident.

In October RB was brought back to fill in for SB who was off sick again. He was made a director in October 2006, a post he kept until November 2007. He made drastic changes to the management team in his first week or two getting rid of PM, the commercial manager and the accountant, KD.

This Dennis Dart, H840 GDY, had a Wadham Stringer Portsdown body. It was photographed in Church Street, Old Town on 17 April 1991 on service 8 from Cherry Gardens Road to Meads. (Alan Snatt)

2007 saw the company in difficulties with the authorities again, this time with the Traffic Commissioners who had surveyed the services and found that too many were running outside their window of being classified as on time – one minute early to five minutes late. Out of 206 timings noted, only 160 were on time. Forty-two were over five minutes late and four were more than a minute early. The company incurred a fine of £25,000 plus costs. An investigation also looked into whether the company was able to reach their standards of financial standing but the company demonstrated that it was compliant, but was fined a further sum of £14,000 (£200 per bus). The maximum it could have been fined was £38,000, but it seems to me to be counter-productive to fine a company that is already in financial difficulties.

SB's health improved and he managed to return to his post.

In 2008, myself and the other shop steward were summoned to the manager's office and were told that the two Conservative members of the Board had resigned. We were also informed that Cariane wanted to sell their 20% holding. The council did not wish to buy them back and had decided to sell their other 80% and were told there were already two interested parties. He wouldn't state who they were but didn't deny they were Go-Ahead, who owned Brighton & Hove, and Stagecoach. He also stated that he did not want Renown/Cavendish to be the purchasers. He expressed his desire that he would like the buses to retain their current livery. We knew that Go-Ahead would probably allow this but Stagecoach would not.

Most of the staff favoured Brighton & Hove to become the new owners. They had an outstation at our depot, had a modern fleet and their staff seemed reasonably content. I wrote to every councillor in the town expressing this point of view. This letter was subsequently leaked to the press.

Our preferences came to nothing as when the envelopes were opened containing the sealed bids, Stagecoach's offer of over £4 million far exceeded the other offer. They also promised to buy twelve new buses and open up their final salary pension scheme to those Eastbourne Buses staff still within the East Sussex County Council's similar scheme.

17th December 2008 was the last day of operation for Eastbourne Buses Ltd. At 4.30pm the two directors left the depot to go to the Town Hall to tender their resignation.

It was a sad day.

STAGECOACH DAYS

The first meeting I had with Stagecoach management was interesting. It was with LW, who had started as a bus conductor and worked his way up through the ranks and was now the Director of Stagecoach UK, one down from Brian Souter, the founder of the company. In front of him on the desk he had a copy of the letter I had sent to the local councillors stating we would rather be taken over by Brighton & Hove. His first words to me were "So you don't want to work for Stagecoach, then." I replied that we were an outstation for Brighton & Hove and they had a good modern fleet and their drivers seemed quite happy whereas nobody has a good word to say about Stagecoach and asked, if he were me, who would he rather work for?

He replied that about five years previously that may have been correct, but it was a much better company to work for now. After the meeting he was shown around the depot and I accompanied him and other managers. LW was a smoker and he asked SB why there was not a smoking shelter on the premises. He replied that it was on his list of things to do. I had to bite my tongue at this because SB had refused all requests for a shelter from the smoking fraternity at the depot. One was subsequently erected.

Part of the deal offered when bidding to buy Eastbourne Buses was to supply 10 new buses. These were Alexander Dennis Enviro300s. (P. Clarke)

Just about fitting under the disused railway bridge at Rotherfield is Volvo Olympian No.359. Before the undergrowth was cleared to the right of the bridge, it made life very exciting as there was no way of knowing what was coming round the sharp bend towards you and it was the site of many near misses.

Not only did Stagecoach buy Eastbourne Buses Ltd, they also purchased Cavendish Motors, part of Renown Coaches, at about the same time. This attracted the attention of the Office of Fair Trading. They declared that no further integration should take place and no more buses should be sprayed in Stagecoach livery. Some Stagecoach directors were even banned from entering the premises. One fact that I never understood was that RB, who had been a director of Eastbourne Buses Ltd and had been a director of the East London Bus Group since January 2009, which became part of the Stagecoach Group again in 2010 when they bought it back from Macquarie Bank after it had gone into administration, also took up a directorship with Renown Coaches between November 2008 and February 2011.

One of the first disciplinaries was for a ticket irregularity spotted by a revenue inspector. We proved that his evidence was incorrect, but the driver was still given an official warning. We appealed this decision and the MD from Stagecoach South Coast was brought in to hear the appeal. He actually upped the award to a final warning. This goes against ACAS guidelines that clearly state that awards should not be increased as it could be seen as a deterrent to appeals and justice. We put in a grievance against this MD for his decision.

This had to be heard by RM, who was in charge of all depots in the south of England. He was initially not allowed onto the premises and had to get permission from the OFT to attend. At our meeting with him, he assured us that the decision was not to be seen as a threat against appeals and agreed it was highly unusual but refused to reverse the decision.

The OFT investigations concluded that the buyout of Eastbourne Buses should be referred to the Monopolies and Mergers Commission, who after spending nearly £230,000 investigating the purchases, decided there was no case to answer.

One of the changes we found noticeable was that where decisions had been made locally in the past, many were now out of the jurisdiction of the depot managers and had to be referred to higher levels, increasing the time of decision making.

Eastbourne Buses had radios fitted to the entire fleet giving drivers direct contact with the depot. With the arrival of their 12 new buses though, this facility came to an end. Stagecoach could not come to an agreement with the suppliers over the cost of supplying and fitting these radios and the existing radios were eventually taken out of service. I would imagine that part of their rationale for removing radios was that if drivers had a phone, they would not need radios. I have never had, or wanted, a mobile phone and this was to lead to

The 'Stagecoach in East Kent' logo on the side of this Volvo Olympian was not strictly correct as it was operating out of Eastbourne's depot in East Sussex when this photo was taken. (Mark Lyons)

problems for me later. However if a driver used his mobile phone to call for assistance while in the cab, even if stationary, he would render himself liable to instant dismissal.

We were using a fleet of four Renault Clios as changeover vehicles. Although only about three years old, they had had a very hard life having over 100 different drivers not treating them with respect. One driver was returning to the depot along Birch Road when he was in collision with a Ford Transit. He was not badly hurt but had a pain in his back, so to be on the safe side, the Fire Brigade took the roof off the car to extricate him. Stagecoach replaced this Clio with a newer Ford Fiesta. About two weeks later another driver tried doing a U turn in Lottbridge Drove and was hit by another car. He, too, hurt his back and the roof had to be cut off that car as well. Management were not amused. I mentioned earlier that Eastbourne Buses were paying nearly £1,000 every day for insurance. Stagecoach keep their costs down by having a £5 million excess on their policy. This means that the cost of the vast majority of accidents is met solely by the company.

The frequency of the service to Tunbridge Wells is owed partly to the running of council contracts to two schools in Tunbridge Wells and one in Heathfield. Here pupils wait in Mayfield on a wet morning for their transport to arrive. Although the Volvo buses were old, they were very reliable and their lives were probably shortened by the need to operate low floor buses. At least one has been preserved.

The entrance to the fire station did not look that steep when we tried turning a bus round at Mayfield due to the road being blocked by a fallen tree. However it grounded and despite our best efforts, we needed professional help to get us mobile again.

Even though all signs of Eastbourne Buses livery had disappeared, the company still legally existed, and the accounts were still filed separately so for the princely sum of £1 the accounts could be downloaded from Companies House. This came in very handy during wage negotiations. I could point out the profits that were being made, the increase in passengers etc. although the Directors would say I should not go by those accounts as they have two sets and I should be referring to the working accounts although I was not privy to these. These negotiations were a bit farcical anyway. I believe that MDs were told how much they could offer and were not allowed to go beyond that figure. We would ballot our members on the offer which would be turned down initially knowing that a slightly improved offer would be made. This would then be accepted because we knew that if we went on strike, staff would be brought in from all over the country to break the strike.

In Eastbourne there are controllers and revenue inspectors who are regularly sent all over the country to break strikes. One was recently even sent to France where a dispute was taking place.

Every depot in Kent and Sussex is treated as a separate entity when it comes to wage negotiations, each with its own rates and conditions. This is so if one depot cannot reach an agreement and decides to strike, then drivers can be brought in from other depots to break the strike. If the negotiations were done as a whole region, then not enough drivers could be found to keep the entire service running should a strike occur.

Even within the Eastbourne Depot, there were different pay rates between ex-Eastbourne Buses staff and ex-Cavendish/new

Two shots that show the perils of driving along Sussex country roads. The car in the distance of the bottom image had pulled out of a side turning. The bus took the engine clean off its chassis before hitting a glancing blow off a tree and veering over the road again and embedding itself into a bank. Nobody was seriously injured but the fire brigade had to cut away the emergency door to release some passengers. The bus, an MAN, was painted white as it was due to be returned to the lessees and they had to be returned in the condition they were received – plain white. (both Mick Gould Recovery)

recruits. Eastbourne Buses staff were paid for their meal breaks and Stagecoach honoured this, but new staff do not get paid for breaks of over 30 minutes, although they are on a slightly higher rate to compensate for this. Bearing in mind some breaks are up to two hours long, the ex-Eastbourne Buses staff have the better deal. I am surprised this has been allowed to continue, but as numbers of these drivers decline with retirements, etc. I think everyone will soon be put on the same contract, even if it means buying them out

Any accident that the company sees as the driver's fault is treated as a "disciplinary" or DP as they are known. This includes the knocking off of wing mirrors which has been the subject of a long running dispute at the Eastbourne depot. Many of the nearside mirrors are on long arms that stick out the front and to the side and are very prone to damage especially on the narrower country roads we have to use. In many places the bus takes up more than half the width of the road so we drive towards the crown of the road. If anything larger than a family saloon comes towards us, we have to pull over causing the mirror to brush against the hedgerow. It is only a matter of luck whether the mirror pushes aside the twigs or hits something more substantial. If the latter is the case, not only does it break the mirror, but often the arm swings round and breaks one of the panes of glass in the entrance door as well. We inherited 10 double deckers from another depot and in the first two weeks of having these, I believe five or six doors were smashed. This is not only expensive but the bus has to be taken out of service and, if in the Rotherfield area where many of these accidents happen, it is about an hour before a relief bus arrives, thus inconveniencing many passengers. We felt that the solution was to fit mirrors that were positioned adjacent to the entrance doors as on other buses. Our engineering manager, PK, refused to do this as it would be contravening the construction and use regulations for that type of vehicle. I could accept that as an answer if similar vehicles at the Hastings depot had not had theirs altered!

I took out one of our '61 reg Scanias on a route 98 to Hastings via Hailsham one quiet Saturday morning. I could not get the nearside mirror to adjust so I could see properly along the nearside of the bus – it was focused on the nearside of the windscreen. I had to stop two or three times on the journey to try to adjust the mirror, but to no avail. In Bexhill Town Centre, I came to the conclusion that it must be the mirror arm that had been bent, so I tried pulling it more to the nearside. Unfortunately instead of bending the arm, it broke the bracket holding it on and the whole assembly came away in my hand. Luckily there was a service 99 behind me and I transferred my passengers. I found a phone box and contacted the Eastbourne depot who asked me to run out of service to Hastings depot to have it fixed. One of their mechanics screwed on a new bracket and refitted the arm. I did point out that it probably wouldn't cure the problem because the arm was bent so he loosened the bolt on the bottom of the hinge and told me to pull the arm out a bit. I tried and it broke his brand new bracket. He said there was only one thing for it and that was to fit a "Hastings type" mirror arm, which he did. Super! I resumed my duty and returned to Eastbourne. A few days later I bumped into PK, and related the story. "I'll have to change that back again," he said, and he did. Mirrors are still regularly being knocked off and drivers are still being disciplined. Whilst defending one driver, whose CCTV footage from the bus clearly saw a vehicle coming towards him, I asked if in future we should have a head-on collision rather than risk a mirror and was met with a stony silence. If a driver has more than one accident in a year, he is put back into the driving school for re-training, which is sensible on the face of it, but accidents include damage to mirrors as well. Also what does not make sense is that they can still continue working until they can be accommodated into the driving school which can be a few weeks if there are a number of new drivers being taught.

On entering the depot one day I was approached by an inspector who said that I had written off a Mercedes whilst driving through Hailsham High Street. That was news to me. I think I might have noticed that so I denied all knowledge of it. The following day I was presented with several photos of an old Mercedes A Class with damage to both offside wheel arches, scuffed alloy wheels, scratched front wing and paint on front corner of bumper. The majority of this damage would have been impossible for me to have done because the offside mirror was still undamaged. The only damage that did match up to damage on the bus I had been driving at the time was the paint on the front bumper which did correspond to paint on the very extreme rear nearside of the bus. This was caused when I pulled into the bus stop layby and went from left hand lock to full right hand lock. This does cause the rear end to swing round very quickly and sharply. Anybody looking at the photos could see that I couldn't possibly could not have caused the vast majority of the damage, but that didn't stop them from accusing me. I have no idea if Stagecoach paid for the entire damage.

Towards the end of my days at Stagecoach I was shop stewarding and had five DPs to defend – all for very minor accidents. All of these were investigated by the Assistant Operations Manager, KK, before progressing to a formal DP with his superior, the Operations Manager.

Two of these had CCTV evidence which showed that no collision had taken place yet the drivers were still sent letters stating they would be disciplined. The first one was thrown out by the OM before we even went in to the hearing as he could see there was no collision. Fair play to him, but this particular driver had just come back from a spell back in the driving school and had been worried sick about his future for the previous week after receiving a letter saying that the outcome of his hearing could result in instant dismissal. I also proved that the other alleged accident did not happen and that was thrown out, but everybody's time could have been saved with a bit of common sense. It makes me wonder how many bus drivers, or lorry drivers come to that, get accused of accidents that have not happened so motorists get their own accident damage fixed for free.

Eastbourne Buses had kept a lot of archives dating back over 100 years. These included old handwritten wages books, financial accounts and a large leather bound book of minutes of management's meetings with the council. These minutes date from 1923 to 1940. They are beautifully handwritten with not a single spelling mistake. There were also a number of bus stop plates, uniforms, old timetables etc. LP said to me one day that he did not trust Stagecoach to look

This Enviro 300 was one of ten promised by Stagecoach when bidding to buy Eastbourne Buses. They were used mainly on the town's busiest 1/1A route which runs from one end of the town to the other. (Mark Lyons)

Stagecoach purchased some Scania/Enviro300s in 2011 and route branded them as "UNOs" for the Service 1, so this one was way off route when spotted in Mayfield on route to Tunbridge Wells.

after them and could I bring them from the stores in the workshop building and put them in a disused office on the top floor of the office block. I enlisted the help of a spare driver and spent the next couple of hours transferring all these archives. We were much happier knowing that the history of Eastbourne Buses was now assured. A little while later though, the depot had a visit from a Stagecoach H&S officer and he was shown around by LP. On looking into the office containing the archives he enquired what it was and LP informed him. His response was simple "Get rid of it!" he said. LP protested that it was the history of the company. He did not care and insisted it should be disposed of. LP asked me if I wanted it. I jumped at the chance. He told me that I was welcome to it but if I was to make any money from it, I was to make a donation to charity. For some years the drivers had put monies that were due back to them from claimed lost property into a fund and items were then purchased for the local hospital. Stagecoach had put an end to this practice, but I put a contribution of £100 to our final donation. I still own this archive.

One of the first changes Stagecoach made was to split the route to Tunbridge Wells into two separate routes. It became a service 52 to Heathfield and then a 252 from there to Tunbridge Wells. The reason for this was, as these were now two routes of about 20 -30 kilometres each, they could come under domestic, rather than European driving rules and tachos did not need to be used. The same bus was used and passengers did not have to change. The only difference was that the driver had to change the destination blind at Heathfield. I was quite happy with this, as I no longer had to keep tachos but it does make a mockery of the law. But that is the fault of highly paid lawmakers in Brussels, rather than Stagecoach.

It seemed that LP was beginning to get more frustrated with Stagecoach's way of doing things – and the reverse was probably true as well. He was the only person on the office side, except for a part time secretary and his work load was exceptional. He confided in me that on one day he had had over 50 emails from his superiors requesting information.

He eventually decided that he did not need the aggravation and left. His position was taken by a younger manager, DB, previously employed by Stagecoach in Scotland. It soon became clear that this manager was struggling as well. He had told us that it had been a bit of a culture shock to him as the depot he had come from had been much larger and he was only responsible for one aspect of management and not expected to deal with anything and everything that came his way as it was at Eastbourne.

He was moved on fairly swiftly and another more experienced manager, BW, moved in. I introduced myself as a union rep in the first couple of days and joked about crossing swords in the future. The good relations did not last too long though.

At the end of his first week, I was working a Service 56 to South Harbour. It was about 18.15 and it was on my last trip of the day. I was about a mile from the end of the route when the bus broke down. It felt as if it had run out of fuel. I apologised to my four passengers and said it may be a while for a relief vehicle to arrive because I did not have any way of contacting the depot. They all said that they were only a couple of stops from home and they decided to walk the rest of the way. The depot was not too far away, and as I did not have a mobile phone, I secured the bus, took my takings and belongings and walked back to the depot taking seven minutes. I informed the controller what had happened to the bus and joined the queue of drivers to use the paying in machine and then went home. My journey home took me past the stricken bus. A mechanic was already on scene, so I stopped and told him the symptoms that caused it to stop and carried on home. The following morning as soon as I walked into the depot, I was stopped by the controller and was told I was suspended from duty and should leave the premises. I asked him why I had been suspended and he just said it was to do with what happened last night but could not elucidate on the exact reason. I went home and informed my full time union officer what had happened. I was not too concerned about being suspended because I was being paid. The thought did cross my mind though was that this could be the new manager trying to make his mark? What better way of getting the drivers into line than by coming down hard on their union rep?

The following Friday I received a telephone call from the Assistant Operations Manager, DR, who told me that they had reconsidered and decided that my actions were not that serious after all, and although still on a disciplinary charge, I could come back to work. Apparently what had happened was that my full time union official, DW, had contacted the MD about the issue and discovered he knew nothing about it. It is Stagecoach policy that he should be informed if any local union officials are suspended, so it was his intervention that led to me being invited back to work.

I eventually attended the disciplinary hearing conducted by BW and defended by DW. It transpired that the controller on duty the evening I broke down had phoned BW and told him I had walked off the job, which was the reason for the suspension, but having viewed the CCTV in the duty room that proved this was not the case. I explained to BW that I did not have a mobile phone so decided that, as the depot was so close, the best option was to return to the depot. BW disagreed though. He thought that I had two better options. Firstly I could have waited for the next bus to come along, flag him down and ask to use his mobile. I disagreed. That potentially would take longer and why should another bus be delayed as I would have to wait for the workshops to be contacted and instructions relayed back to me. His other option was for me to go into the Kentucky Fried Chicken restaurant opposite and ask the floor manager if I could use their phone. I could not believe he put this forward as a serious option. Floor manager! In the posh restaurants where Stagecoach executives dine they may well have floor managers, but this was a Kentucky. I also asked him why other companies in the town were expected to supply a communications system to the depot when they would not supply one for themselves. Also, did he expect the person serving to desert his duties to lead me to their phone, which was probably behind the counter, thereby breaking Health & Safety rules as I would be improperly dressed. I thought my defence had gone very well when we adjourned for BW to consider his decision. On our return though, BW declared that I should not have left the vehicle unattended and that I had better options rather than returning to the depot and awarded me a Final Warning but told me I could appeal his decision. I most certainly did.

This appeal was held in front of the Director of Operations, NI. DW defended me again. You cannot accuse management of not being thorough in their disciplinaries and we went through every detail of the events again. I asked why the mechanic had not been disciplined. He could not fix the bus and had left it unattended for about an hour before it was towed in. He could not answer. I also asked if a bus broke down in the road outside the depot, could I walk back into the depot to report it or would I have to go into one of the factories adjacent or opposite the depot to ask to use their phone. He said if that was the case I could of course return to the depot, so I then asked where the invisible line was on the road that marked the boundary to being OK to return to the depot and being a disciplinary offence. He said he could not answer that; indeed no manager would be able to answer that, so I asked him if management didn't know where this line was, how could a driver be expected to know. Again there was no answer. Stagecoach managers and directors are not very good at answering hypothetical questions but are very good at appointing blame after that situation has occurred. I think they must have all attended the University of Stagecoach and obtained first class honours degrees in "Being Wise After The Event". We adjourned again and on our return NI declared that my Final Warning had been commuted to a Caution.

Stagecoach transferred five Dennis Tridents, 18172-76, from Kent. 18175 was photographed with me driving southbound at Mayfield.

I was still not happy with this outcome but could not take it further because the Disciplinary Agreement precludes minor awards being appealed as far as the MD. DW was not happy either and stated that he thought that I had been singled out as I was a union rep and he would be taking it further. In the meantime I put in a grievance that I had been unfairly treated because I was a union rep. Grievances about disciplinary outcomes were not allowed as a rule, but the MD, PM, decided that he would hear this one. DW again attended and we put our case. PM stated that he could not overturn a disciplinary result so I said he could make a ruling that the case should never have been brought in the first place, which he declined to do. The meeting finished without an agreement and DW was as good as his word and the Unite Union took Stagecoach to an industrial tribunal over the case.

The hearing was held at Brighton. I was shown into a room where I met my defence barrister, a lady who had travelled down from London. DW also attended. In the room on the other side of the corridor were the MD, PM, the Director of Operations, NI, the depot's Operation's Manager, BW, his assistant, DR, and their legal representatives. I briefed my defence who then said "You're not expecting to win this, are you?"

She went on to say that Stagecoach could agree that I had been treated harshly, but say they treat all their staff just as harshly and

I hope this driver was not spotted by a road inspector as it is against the rules to drive whilst wearing a Hi-Vis jacket. The bus was photographed leaving Shinewater Estate on its way into town. (Mark Lyons)

this would be a good defence as it was up to me to prove I was treated differently to other staff. I said I had been treated differently because the mechanic who attended the bus also left it there and for much longer than I had and was not disciplined at all.

It was about this stage that a court official entered the room and said there had been a bit of a blunder as it had only just been realised that the case was down to be heard by a single judge, but it should also be heard in front of two lay members as well – one from union side and one from management – to advise the judge and it would be some time before these two could make it to the court. He said that another case had been scheduled to be heard that day, so that one would be heard first. He went on to say that I had a choice of waiting and starting the case later in the day, but there would not be time to finish it or I could cancel it and come back a different day. I could see no value in only hearing part of it, so opted for the latter. Both sides were then told to go to into the court room to fix a mutually agreed date for the future hearing. This created a problem for the MD as he had been posted to a different depot up north. Whilst waiting outside the courtroom, he mentioned how smart I was looking that day. I replied that that was because I was not wearing the company's awful uniform! I sat next to him in the court while a new date, in about three or four weeks' time, was agreed. The judge then said that the court in Brighton was closing before the agreed date and we would all have to go to Havant, near Portsmouth. As we left the courtroom, I said to the MD that it was ridiculous that it had got this far as all I did was report that one of their buses had broken down. He sent one of his team into our room and said they were prepared to settle the case by taking the disciplinary from my record that evening and donating £250 to a charity of my choice.

After a bit of thought and with my brief's words about not expecting to win still uppermost in my mind, I responded by saying that if they upped their charitable donation to £500, I would settle. They refused and said it was £250 or nothing. Both my parents had just died of cancer so I eventually agreed and Cancer UK benefitted from the debacle.

Whilst waiting for the tribunal case to come to court, I was working another trip to Tunbridge Wells. Between Five Ashes and Mayfield, the A267 is an accident black spot which includes a steep downhill stretch followed by a similar uphill section. There are double white lines in the centre of the road as there are many hidden entrances. I was driving a second hand DAF double decker that Eastbourne Buses had bought from a firm in Manchester that had had their operator's licence revoked. They were never nice to drive

Stagecoach kept and repainted some buses owned by Eastbourne Buses. An example of this was a DAF Cadet with Wright bodywork, unusually seen out of town at Heathfield bound for Tunbridge Wells.

at the best of times. Whilst going down the hill, I thought it was going very well even though I did not have my foot on the throttle and thought it may have stuck open. Going up the other side needed full throttle and as it was a dangerous place to stop I carried on uphill into Mayfield village. To check the throttle I selected neutral and the revs went through the roof. I managed to shut the engine down, waited a minute and tried again. Once more the revs went sky high. I shut it down again and phoned the depot from the phone box in the village. After about an hour, a mechanic arrived and got out of his van clutching a box of springs. "I know what's wrong with this" he declared, "The spring we put on the throttle return has snapped". He lifted the engine hatch and he was right. Two halves of a very weak spring were dangling from their securing points. I said "Do you mean to tell me that this bus was sent out knowing that at some time there was a good chance the throttle would stick open." He agreed they had. The workshops were waiting for a spare part to arrive and the spring was a temporary fix though clearly not up to the job. He fitted a stronger one and I returned the bus to the depot, where I went ballistic. The managers could not defend their actions and assured me it would be fixed properly before it went back on the road again.

Relations with BW improved after that. Like other managers though, he was beginning to feel the pressure of the job and was taking more time off sick.

Eventually BW left and was replaced by RT, the youngest manager, I've ever worked with. He was still in his twenties and was a stickler for the rules. I once said to him "Rules are for the guidance of wise men and the obedience of fools" but it didn't seem to have any effect on his decision making. He blindly stuck to the rulebook.

The first instance we encountered of this blinkered view was when the senior driver, KD, who had started in 1970, had to phone the depot because of a fault on his bus. Not being allowed to use a mobile in his cab, he followed procedure and got out of his cab making the call from the pavement. Unseen by him though, a bundle of notes had fallen from his cash tray and was lying on the bus floor. A passenger spotted this, left his seat, picked up the notes and left the bus. There was over £100 involved. We are responsible for our takings, so KD knew he would have to pay it back from his own pocket. He reported the incident when he returned to the depot. What did RT do? He suspended him for not looking after company property! The other shop steward, JE, and I went in to see RT and asked him why he had suspended the driver. He told us he was amazed that we were even questioning his decision. KD had clearly broken the rules. We said we were amazed as well. KD could not have been feeling great. He had just been robbed, knew he had to pay back over £100 and instead of being shown a bit of sympathy, he was now suspended. A couple of days later the Director of Operations, NI, was visiting the depot and I went to see him relaying him the story. To his credit this time, he could see we were correct and no further action was taken against KD.

Knowing RT stuck to the rules could work in our favour though. One driver had refused to give a girl a child fare even though she produced a passport to prove her age. I don't understand why some drivers make life so difficult for themselves. If someone asked for a child fare I would give them what they asked for because management invariably would not back a driver up if they were wrong. Anyway at his DP, he was asked to explain his actions. He said that rules stated that 15 years olds must have a Stagecoach ID pass, not a passport and he was simply following the company's rules. RT amazingly agreed and the case was dismissed, although common sense would have found him guilty.

Ticket irregularities, or fiddling to be blunt, are taken very seriously, and quite rightly so, but sometimes things are not as they first appear. I was working a very busy 98 between Hailsham and Hastings one morning rush hour. By the time I reached Ninfield, I was about 10 minutes late. The last person in the queue wanted a single to Bexhill, which was £1 10p at the time and gave me a £10 note. I issued his ticket and gave him his change. The first person at the next stop also had a £10 note for a Day Rider which was just over £3. Again I issued a ticket and gave him his change. He looked at the ticket he had just taken from the machine and declared "This is a £1 10p ticket"

"It can't be," I replied, but when he showed it to me it was. I then realised what had happened. The passenger who had bought the single ticket at the previous stop had been concentrating more on getting his change than taking his ticket and had forgotten to do so. The ticket machines are angled in such a way that issued tickets are not always visible to the driver. They were also getting old and in need of maintenance and the buttons do not always work first time and the Day Rider, I thought I had issued to the second passenger, had not come from the machine and he had taken the single ticket meant for the previous passenger. I took this ticket from him and issued the correct one. I am grateful for that passenger for being so diligent because if he had tried to board another bus later that day with a single ticket, his entry would have been refused. If he then quite rightly complained to the company, that ticket would have been traced to me and by that time I would have had no explanation of what had happened.

A couple of weeks later another driver was on a final appeal for a ticket irregularity and both the MD and OD were at the depot. I went to see them and related my story saying that although it was not directly connected to the case, it was a good example of how easy it is to make an honest mistake. I suggested that if my passenger had complained, I would probably be facing dismissal. They both agreed, even though at that time I had a forty year unblemished record when it came to honesty.

One of the most bizarre incidents happened under RT's watch. A driver, DH, was heading north to Tunbridge Wells. As he approached the bus stop in Mayfield village, a black BMW was parked on the bus stop. He pulled up alongside to board his one intending passenger. The driver of the BMW was in his car and was ready to go and was annoyed at being boxed in. As the bus drove off and then went down the narrow lane towards the A267, the BMW over took him at speed. At the junction the driver got out, put up his bonnet and was looking at his engine as if he had a problem. DH slowed down and assessed that there was just enough room between the BMW and the bollard to drive through. This seemingly annoyed the BMW driver as he thought he had totally blocked the road, so he threw himself against the side of the bus as if he had been hit. DH thought this behaviour totally irrational and did not want to put himself or his passengers in any danger, so carried on. The car driver shut his bonnet, got back in his car and returned to Mayfield. To cover himself, DH reported the incident to the police, as technically he had been in an accident with a pedestrian, and had not exchanged details. The police took no action. On his return to the depot, he also put in a report to the management. It took them nearly two weeks to view the CCTV, upon which they suspended him and then sacked him summarily for failing to exchange details. We were stunned. We appealed to the Director of Operations, NI. We argued that the handbook states that we should not rise to acts of provocation and, if pretending to break down to lure the driver from his cab was not an act of provocation, then deliberately throwing himself against the side of the bus, definitely was. We also pointed out that if DH had not reported the incident, management would not know anything about it because the BMW driver did not lodge a complaint. All our arguments fell on deaf ears and the decision to sack him was upheld. Unbelievable! Although DH had found employment with another bus company, we persuaded him to carry on with the appeal process with a final plea to the MD, PN. At this hearing, the whole case was thrown out completely which surprised us, because normally when an appeal is won, the award is downgraded to a written or final warning and part of the punishment is that although the driver is invited back, they are not paid between his initial sacking and winning the appeal, but in this case he was also paid for this period. DH understandably did not wish to return to a company that had treated him so badly,

Ex No.52 Leyland Olympian was sold to Harris Bus of Grays and eventually found its way to East Yorkshire.

but now his CV reads that he resigned from Stagecoach rather than was sacked. At a Stagecoach long service awards dinner that I was invited to, I approached the MD and said that although we do not normally "talk shop" at these awards, I thanked him for giving DH his job back. His reply was "No brainer, Wasn't it?"

Another case where a driver found a new employer whilst awaiting an appeal against dismissal entailed GB. He had volunteered, with another driver from the Eastbourne depot, to work temporarily at Exeter, where the company was very short of staff. He had been there a couple of weeks, when the area was hit by floods. He had to run out of service back to the depot down a lane that he had been told was flooded and manhole covers may have been dislodged. To cover himself, he lodged his mobile phone or other camera, between his personal bag and the windscreen and filmed his journey which, as it turned out, was fairly uneventful. He phoned his partner that evening, as he usually did, and asked if she wanted to view the footage. He uploaded the footage on to his Facebook page with a comment that if we found our route 252 tricky, we should try this one. Somebody, who was not averse to enhancing their career prospects at the expense of others, reported this to management. In my opinion, the company is verging on paranoia when it comes to bad publicity. They actually employ someone at their head office in Perth to monitor social media. Anyway, the driver was recalled from Exeter. At his DP, at which he was accompanied by another shop steward, he was somewhat vociferous in his defence. They sacked him, but he soon found employment with another local bus company. He appealed though, and I represented him. In the meantime I had been told by the AOM, and by a controller who had been told to find him work in Eastbourne from the following day, that RT had no intention to sack him as being recalled to Eastbourne would be punishment enough, but was sacked because of what he had said at his hearing.

I used this information at his appeal. NI also had a written print out of subsequent comments made on his GB's Facebook page. I asked him which of the comments had brought the company into disrepute. He couldn't tell me. I said that he if could not tell me what he had specifically said, then how could I possibly defend him. Again there was no answer. We adjourned and on our return his award was reduced to a final warning. In effect, this means that any incident that occurs in the next 18 months that you are found guilty of, is liable to mean dismissal. Not many staff manage this and the pressure put upon drivers every day they report for duty is enormous. For example, many bus stops are near junctions and if, when pulling away, an intending passenger runs around the corner, do you stop and pick them up? Drivers have a responsibility to other road users as well as passengers, but if the passenger complains, it could lead to your dismissal. GB went home after his appeal, but returned in the evening with all his Stagecoach uniform, emergency tickets etc. and handed in his notice. Again his CV reads he resigned rather than was sacked. That was another experienced bus driver the company had lost. Turnover of staff was very high. Last time I checked, nearly 50% of staff had only been there for about three years or less and that does not take into account those who had started and left within that time.

An example of a driver spectacularly failing to reach 18 months on a final warning is this next story. This was DE. He had a terrible record and I was defending him again one day. Both of us expected him to get the sack. He lived in Uckfield and was so sure he would lose his job, he had brought his partner with him so they could spend the rest of the day in town. To both our surprise he got away with a final warning. This gave him a problem as his partner was now stranded in Eastbourne. A call came in to the depot from a driver who had broken down in Tunbridge Wells and DE was told to grab a spare bus and go to Tunbridge Wells to do a change over. DE saw this as an opportunity to take his partner home, so he went via Uckfield. Not only that but he stopped at a café on the way and bought a sandwich

Retirement ceremony. That's me on the left.

and cup of coffee. He ate the sandwich before continuing on his way drinking the coffee while on the move. All this was recorded on CCTV which management downloaded to see why he was so late in reaching Tunbridge Wells. I advised him to resign - he did !

It must be said, though, in many ways, Stagecoach are good employers. Most of the routes are capable of being run on time without too much difficulty although there are many daily events beyond their control that make buses late. The fleet is kept in good order and I believe every vehicle has to be serviced every three weeks or it cannot be used. In Eastbourne Buses days they were serviced every four weeks. Payment of wages is assured and there is a good pension scheme, although the final salary scheme has closed. Shares are available to purchase with the company adding shares to those purchased by staff. From a passenger's point of view, a good level

The last new buses to arrive at Eastbourne while I was there were two Scania Enviro400s to be used on the "Wave" route to Hastings so this was another bus "off route" at Mayfield.

of service is operated – the service to Tunbridge Wells is now every 30 minutes compared to hourly in the Eastbourne Buses era. Brian Souter, the founder, seems to have found a way to make a profit from running bus services and this formula seems to have to be adhered to. Where I differ from their approach is the way staff are treated on a daily basis. Drivers are not all angels and do some stupid things, but I think that often a "quiet word" in a driver's ear would have better results than a formal disciplinary. Passengers appreciate a friendly face when they board a bus and many drivers are unhappy over the way they, or their workmates, are being treated.

Safety is, of course, treated as paramount, partly because accidents cost money. A few years ago a system called Greenroad was fitted in every cab. This monitors how the bus is being driven. Every driver has to "tap in" to the system when taking over a bus. Four disciplines are then monitored – acceleration, braking, cornering and changing lanes. A unit with red, amber and green lights is mounted in the cabs out of sight of the general public. The idea is for the driver to keep the light on green. If braking is too hard or if a corner is taken too sharply then an "event" is triggered and the amber light flashes. Harder braking triggers the red light. These are also recorded. Drivers are allowed twenty events every ten hours. If a driver keeps his score below twenty for four complete consecutive weeks they earn a bonus of £5. It is very difficult not to score an event. If, on approaching a traffic light, it turns to amber and one brakes normally and safely, then the amber light flashes. This encourages drivers to keep going. Similarly if overtaking a parked car, a vehicle appears from the other direction, then pulling over to give way will undoubtedly lead to another event. More passengers who are running for buses are being left behind for the same reason.

Drivers can check on line to see how they have fared. Exact times, places and type of event are recorded and drivers can see how well they are doing compared to other drivers within the depot. Depots are also compared with each other. I must admit I was quite good at this. I imagined a ball bearing was sitting in the bottom of a bowl and I tried to keep it there. I only managed to go for a whole week with getting a single event once. This system means that some drivers make no effort to get back on time if running late as that would probably impact on their Greenroad score. The system is supposed to save fuel, but when I asked the Engineering Manager, he said there had been no noticeable savings. It is difficult to say if there are any fewer accidents because of it. It can be used to the drivers' advantage though, as any complaints about rough rides or braking too hard can be defended by referring to Greenroad.

Luckily road rage incidents are rare, but two cases spring to mind. The first was when I was travelling into town along Seaside. I stopped at a red traffic light behind another car. He did not notice when the lights changed to green, so I gave him a polite toot on the horn. He pulled away, but was obviously annoyed at me because he kept his speed to less than 10 mph although he had a clear road ahead. Seeing an opportunity to overtake, I pulled out, so he accelerated. I pulled in behind him again and he slammed his brakes on causing me to brake hard. He had two young children in the back of his car as well. I had to stop at the next bus stop and he disappeared up the road. I thought that would be the end of the matter, but in the town centre I noticed him waiting to come out of a T junction. I stopped with my bus blocking his exit, got out of the cab and walked towards his car. I ignored him though, instead speaking to his lady passenger, saying that if they were her kids in the back of the car, they deserved better than him and walked away. I thought it would be far more effective if she gave him an ear-bashing all afternoon!

The second case did not actually involve me, but I witnessed two other motorists having an argument. Suddenly one gave the other a left hook and a minor scuffle ensued. As I have often been grateful to have had witnesses in the past I gave my details to the guy who had been hit. It actually got to court and I was called as a witness. After I had given my evidence I was allowed to stay in court which I did. I was quite shocked to hear a policemen relate to the female judge in the most explicit language you can possibly imagine the exact words of the defendant. He was also accused of kicking the plaintiff which I had not witnessed. During a recess, quite bizarrely I walked out beside the defendant and remember telling him he should not have defended himself but got professional help as I had not witnessed the alleged kick. He was not unduly antagonistic towards me but that was before he had been hit with a fine and costs amounting to over £1,000.

Every so often, the depots are visited unannounced by company auditors. They are treated like Gods and they go through all systems within the depot and if managers do not reached a certain standard, they are in bother. It is undoubtedly a very stressful time for them. Drivers are checked as well, with auditors sitting on roadsides checking bus times. They even arrive early in the morning and check buses as they leave the depot to make sure that they are on time and drivers have filled in their Defect Card. It is a legal requirement to complete this form after doing a walk round safety check of their vehicle. One morning I was in a queue of five buses waiting to leave. By the time I had reached the auditor I was two minutes late. I was asked why I was late. I told him it was his fault as I was on time when I joined the queue. He said that was OK and I could go. "Aren't you going to make a note of why I'm late?" I enquired "You have when everybody else was late". He declined and told me to go.

Stagecoach are very good with their systems of work. As an H&S officer, I was taken off the road every week to do a walk round check of the depot at Birch Road and offices at Cornfield Road. I had a form to complete and make a couple of copies of it. Hot and cold water temperatures are checked as well as visual checks on cleanliness etc. Doing these checks did not mean that any faults were fixed with any expediency though, but the paperwork had been done.

There were also two large files for Risk Assessments and Safe Systems of Work. These have to be updated and signed off every few years. Although some of the more important ones, such as reversing buses in the yard, are posted for drivers to see, many are not. I can only speak for the Eastbourne depot, although I suspect it is the same elsewhere, but I doubt if many drivers know they are not supposed to have their bags beside them in the cabs or even more surprisingly they should not set off the panic alarms fitted to buses if they are being attacked, as this may enrage their attacker even more! Another one recommends that those driving a company car should take a break every two hours, but bus drivers are regularly expected to drive for five hours without a break. All these files are kept in the OM's office.

Another waste of everybody's time are CPCs which are the European Government's idea. These are courses that bus drivers have to undergo in order to keep their licences. On the face of it, it is a good idea that bus drivers should be retrained. Drivers have to do five days in the classroom spread over five years. There are a number of different courses including driving assessments, disablement awareness and customer service. So why do I think they are a waste of time? Because drivers do not have to complete every module in five years. They can do the same one five times. Indeed the last course I went on there was a lady who was doing the disablement awareness course for the fifth time in about the last year. This qualified her for a further five years of bus driving. They are also a waste of time because most courses could be taught in far less than one day. For example, the last course I attended with five other drivers, the morning session up to a tea break was taken up by the attendees giving three "facts" about themselves, but one had to be made up and the rest of the class had to try to guess which fact was made up. What has that got to do with being disabled?

LAST DAYS

During my last few months at work I had let it be known to RT that after my retirement I would like to stay on driving on a casual basis as other drivers did. This meant that you only worked if they were short of staff but I saw it as a good way of winding down from full time employment. He had no objection to this. Before I retired though, RT handed in his notice to go to work for Arriva. The manager from the Hastings depot, RH, took temporary charge and he also had no objections if I stayed on.

A notice to staff was posted advertising the post of Operations Manager due to the promotion of RT. We all knew he hadn't been promoted, unless of course, Stagecoach Directors think that being a manager for a rival company is promotion. The Assistant Operations Manager, KK, applied for the post.

On my last day of service I was relieved from duty so I could say goodbye to my work colleagues. Most of my mates from Eastbourne Buses days had already retired or left and many of the others had only been there a short while and I had not really got to know them, so I took the opportunity to go over some of the Health and Safety procedures with DT who was taking over the role from me.

About 2 pm, I was called into the office by KK. I was asked if this was my last day. Taken somewhat aback by this question, especially as earlier in the morning he had handed me a leaving interview questionnaire), I concurred that it was. He then told me I would have to hand in my float, emergency tickets, cash tray, etc. I told him that I was going to stay on a casual driver, so would still need them. He then dropped the bombshell that he did not intend using casual staff and re-iterated that I was to hand in my gear. I protested somewhat vociferously!

I asked him if he intended keeping GP on as a casual driver. He affirmed that he was. When I asked why, he told me that GP was reliable. I protested even more. Since I have been with my present partner – about 20 years, I have had one spell off work when I needed a minor operation, had not been late, had no costly accidents or had any justifiable complaints from the public. I said that I lived within 10 minutes from the depot and would be available for call out at short notice. How much more reliable did he want? There was no persuading him though. He had made his mind up. I said goodbye to the controllers in their office and stormed out. Not the way I envisaged leaving after 44 years would be like.

I walked through my front door to balloons and decorations put up by my partner wishing me a happy retirement. I was in no mood to celebrate though. I sat down and penned a not too complimentary letter to the MD, PN. I also wrote an article for the local paper with the heading "Acrimonious Retirement of Bus Driver, Mick" knowing that one thing Stagecoach is paranoid about is bad publicity. I refrained from sending it though until PN had time to respond to my letter. After a week or so of silence from the company, I contacted my full time Union Officer, DW, who agreed to take up my case. A few days later DW phoned to say that he had spoken to PN who would be in touch with me. I waited another 10 days and despite an email from me saying I would like an answer, still no word from PN.

By this time I was quite enjoying my retirement and not missing driving buses as much as I thought I would. I had even been offered a job by a local coaching firm saying they would like me to do perhaps one or two days a week on a casual basis. It seemed quite tempting.

Annoyed that PN had ignored my correspondence, I emailed my letter to the local paper. You guessed it. Three days later and before any article was published – if indeed they intended publishing it, a letter dropped through my door from Stagecoach! The MD had objected to the way I had written about his new manager – I think he was referring to my phrase "devoid of any management skills" and then said he thought I had misunderstood what he had meant.

Although the new manager, KK, was Polish, I think it is difficult to misunderstand "Hand in your gear. We do not employ casual staff." The MD did say in his letter that that he would be happy to have me back on a casual basis. Oh, dear. What to do now? I spent the weekend thinking about it.

In the end I decided to go back, partly because I wanted to smile sweetly at KK when I saw him again and partly because I had earnt an attendance bonus for not going sick during 2016 which was paid out during March and I wanted to make sure I received it. An apologetic phone call was needed to the local rag asking them to ignore the letter I had sent denigrating the company. They fully understood the situation and did not print it. It did cross my mind that a reporter had contacted Stagecoach for their side of the story and as they detest bad publicity wrote to me swiftly, but I have no proof either way. The timing was suspicious though.

I went back to see KK and he re-iterated that I was not on their books as a casual driver as he already had three and named them. I told him that one of the names, PP, who had already retired had gone back to his home town of Southampton. He told me that he would call me if I was needed but again said that I still had to hand in my emergency tickets, float, gear etc.

I have not received a call and don't expect to.

RETIREMENT

I am thoroughly enjoying my freedom. My large model railway is being expanded, I have taken up drawing again, I am keeping fit by trying to walk every day and I have been writing these memoirs.

Reading back through them, it sounds as if I was a right troublemaker, but please bear in mind those events took place over 44 years. On the vast majority of days, I arrived on time and had an uneventful day.

Two questions remain though. Firstly, if I could go back 44 years, would I still walk into the depot in Churchdale Road and apply for a job? The answer is yes, I probably would.

The second question, knowing what they know now, would they employ me? I'm afraid that question will have to go unanswered!

Retirement certificate.